Writers Like Us:
My Life with Sinclair Lewis

Barnaby Conrad

with Barnaby Conrad III

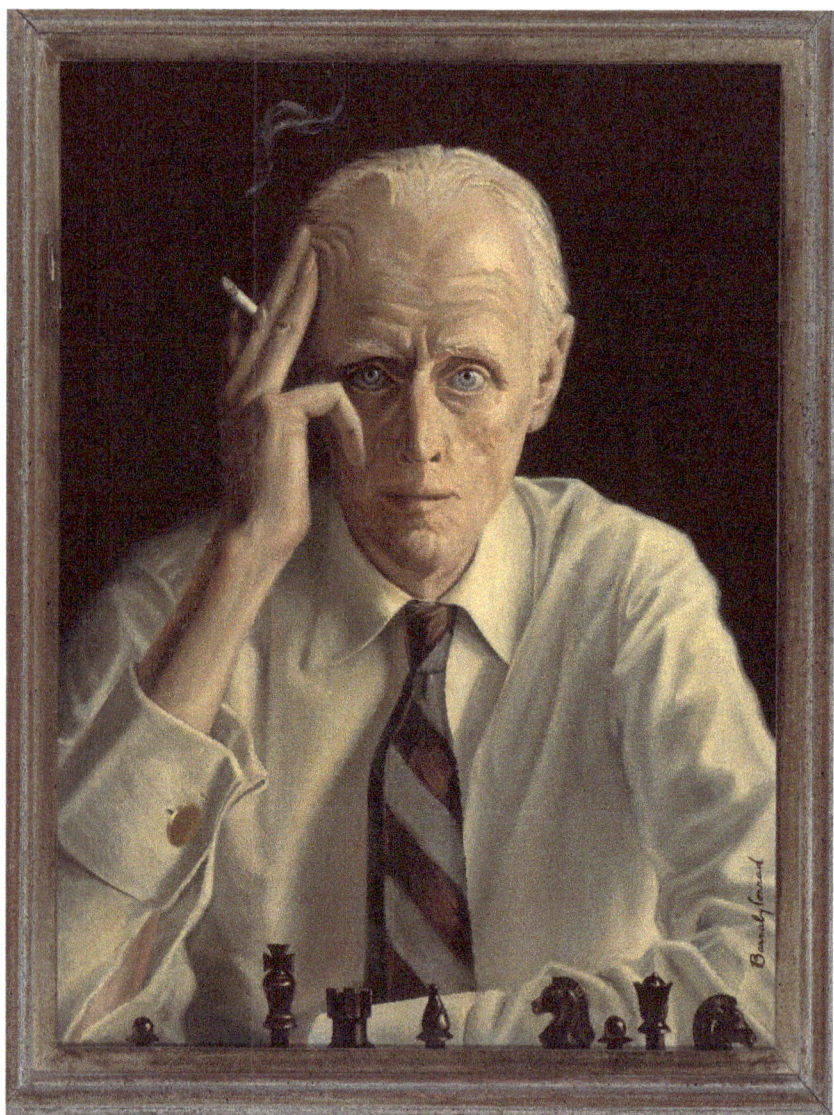

Sinclair Lewis, 1950 by Barnaby Conrad.
Collection of the Ransom Center, University of Texas.

Writers Like Us:
My Life with Sinclair Lewis

Barnaby Conrad

with Barnaby Conrad III

Academica Press
Washington~London

Library of Congress Cataloging-in-Publication Data
Names: Conrad, Barnaby (author) | Conrad III, Barnaby (editor)
Title: Writers like us : my life with sinclair lewis | Conrad, Barnaby.
Description: Washington : Academica Press, 2025. | Includes references.
Identifiers: LCCN 2024952151 | ISBN 9781680534207 (hardcover) |
9781680534221 (paperback) | 9781680534214 (e-book)

For Martha and Jack

Contents

FOREWORD

In the summer of 1947 Sinclair Lewis, America's first winner of the Nobel Prize for Literature, hired my father to serve as his personal secretary for four months. In the twilight of his career, Lewis, at sixty-two, was an unpredictable, opinionated genius who left an enormous impression on everyone he met, especially on my then twenty-five-year-old father.

Over the next six decades Dad wrote about Lewis both in short memoir and fiction. In 2010, I suggested he write something longer about his mentor, pointing out that he was the last person alive who knew Lewis well. Though intrigued by the idea, my father worried that at age eighty-eight, he wasn't quite up to the task. I volunteered to research overlooked letters, supply biographical facts, and correct previous errors, while my father added new material (in his looping longhand) to the growing sheaf of pages.

Newly-surfaced letters added depth to Dad's efforts, but they sometimes contradicted details from his 1969 memoir, *Fun While It Lasted* (certainly a liability of the genre). I also chose to include more biographical material about Lewis's life up to his death in 1951. We had a hundred and twenty pages of manuscript when my father died at age ninety in February 2013; I vowed to complete the mission.

Nearly all artists and writers begin an apprenticeship by copying their chosen master's style. I learned to write from my father, and though we diverged stylistically over the years, as the editor of this memoir I've done my best to stay true to his literary voice and to fulfill his intentions. — *Barnaby Conrad III*

ACKNOWLEDGEMENTS

Librarian Tom Steman of Saint Cloud State University in Minnesota provided swift access to hundreds of letters written by Sinclair Lewis to Marcella Powers between 1939 to 1949, as well as correspondence between Lewis, Ida Kay Compton, and my father. Sally E. Parry of the Sinclair Lewis Society offered editing and encouragement. I am indebted to the Beinecke Library at Yale, which houses the papers of Sinclair Lewis and of my father. Thanks to the Ransom Center at the University of Texas, which owns my father's oil portrait of Sinclair Lewis. The Chicago Public Library provided letters between Horace Cayton, Jr., Ida Kay Compton, and my father. The Lewis biographies by Mark Schorer and by Richard Lingeman were essential. Mark Hugh Miller, Matthew Palmieri, John Ross Bush, and Jeffrey Meyers provided insightful editing. Thanks to literary agent Cristina Concepcion, editor Paul du Quenoy, and designer Soumyadev Bose for bringing the book to print.

Finally, I am grateful to my wife Martha Sutherland for her affectionate patience in handling three generations of Conrad men. — Barnaby Conrad III

CHAPTER ONE

SANTA BARBARA STREET

"Red Lewis is out your way—give him a call." So read the note from Marcella Powers, my literary agent in New York. It was mid-March 1947, and Sinclair Lewis, the first American to win the Nobel Prize in Literature, was renting a bungalow on Anacapa Street, not far from my parents' house in Santa Barbara.

After leaving Yale in the fall of 1943 and serving two years as a Vice Consul in war-time Spain, I'd spent six months writing and portrait painting in Lima, Peru, where I made a little extra money playing cocktail piano at the best hotel in town. Marcella had managed to sell a few of my bullfighting articles to *Esquire* and *True*, but I was now twenty-five and living at home, trying to write a first novel. I wanted very much to meet Sinclair Lewis, but I couldn't imagine such a literary giant being interested in me.

Though I'd read many of Lewis's books, I much preferred Fitzgerald, Hemingway, and James M. Cain, authors who wrote about romance, war, and crime. While the press interviewed him constantly, Lewis seemed a man of letters from another era; yet his impudent, cantankerous remarks on politics and mankind's foibles intrigued me. More to the point, I hankered after fame and fortune and Sinclair Lewis was the richest author in America. What did I have to lose?

So, on my way to teach Spanish at the Cate School I drove by Lewis's rented house on Anacapa Street hoping to simply bump into the author of *Main Street*. When a second note from Marcella announced that "Red" Lewis was soon heading down to Hollywood to discuss his novel, *Cass Timberlane* for the screen, I knew it was now or never. I scrawled three rough drafts to compose this note:

Dear Mr. Lewis:

I am an embryonic writer. I would like to meet you for no other purpose than to meet you. I realize how busy you are but if there were a free moment before you leave, I would consider it a rare privilege to be able to drop over and…

I only briefly mentioned my agent. Newly married and still in her late twenties, Marcella Powers had been Sinclair Lewis's mistress for almost eight years, and I was unsure of their current relationship. I sealed the envelope, walked to 2535 Anacapa Street, and dropped it into his mailbox.

The following day at noon the doorbell rang at my parents' house. I swung the door open to find a heavyset black man in livery standing at the threshold. He slowly removed his hat. "I'm Joseph Hardrick, chauffeur to Mr. Lewis." Behind him in the driveway purred an elegant sedan; I wondered if Sinclair Lewis was sitting in the shadowy back seat.

"Mr. Lewis would like you to come to tea at five o'clock," said Hardrick.

"Tomorrow?"

"Today."

"Wow. That would be fine," I managed. "Thank you."

After the chauffeur nodded and left, I was flooded with excitement, trying to imagine what to say to the great Sinclair Lewis. In preparation, I pulled a couple of his books from my parents' library, skimming the pages of *Main Street* and *Babbitt*. They were set in the Midwest, a region I knew only as prairie vistas through the windows of a New York-bound train in my not-so-long-ago years at Yale. Then I picked up *Elmer Gantry* with its boldly blunt first sentence: "Elmer Gantry was drunk." After reading Spanish for three years in Spain and Peru, I was struck by the *Americanness* of Lewis's Midwestern subject and style. I finally put the books down—I wasn't cramming for an exam, was I?—and went back to typing my own novel. As I polished up a colorful scene about an old gypsy woman begging in Málaga, I imagined the book becoming as big a hit as one of Sinclair Lewis's. After all, Andalusía trumped the homespun prairie for romance, no?

That evening, in a suit and tie, I walked the few blocks to the palm-shaded house on Anacapa Street and bounced up the front steps. Before I could ring the bell, the door opened and Joseph Hardrick ushered me into the living room. "He'll be with you shortly."

I sat down on the sofa and looked around. It was a comfortable dwelling that George F. Babbitt might have called "well-appointed," but the living room smelled like a giant ashtray. Everyone smoked in those days. While I waited for Mr. Lewis, I noticed a black binder on the cocktail table, looking terribly fat and interesting. An adhesive label bore the odd title, *Ebenezer*. Next to it lay a copy of Plato's *Republic*.

A high-pitched Midwestern voice boomed, "How d'ye do!"

I stood up as a tall, red-faced scarecrow in a baggy tweed suit lurched into the room with his head back and his skeletal hand held high, as if reaching for the bridle of a skittish mule. He gripped my hand with an awkward yet exhilarating crunch. Sinclair Lewis was a startling sight at sixty-two. His once blazing red hair was now thin and orangey-white, and his buck teeth were stained yellow from tobacco. I recoiled from the haunted blue eyes sunk into a scarlet face that was ravaged and scarred, pocked and cratered from countless operations for skin cancer. He was fiercely ugly, quite the ugliest person I had ever seen.

Yet ten minutes after meeting him—when he started to talk and ramble—I no longer thought him ugly. He was kind and rapacious, charming and cutting, factual and fanciful, reverent and irreverent, profound and gossipy. I was no longer aware of that blistered red face, just of a powerful personality, a towering imagination expressed with boyish enthusiasm. We talked of all manner of things. I learned later that this was a talking period for him, a lonely time. Subsequently, I would come to know his long silent periods; both were equally compulsive.

He fumbled a cigarette from a crumpled package and stuck it—bent—in his mouth. The words spilled out him: "So you're a writer, eh? And a Yale man, to boot! Marcella tipped me off. I remember way back when I was at Yale—dreadful place—and I said to Professor Tinker—y'know, the great Tink—that I wanted to be a writer and nothing but a writer, and he said, 'But you'll starve,' and I said, 'Don't care if I do,' and he said, 'Then you'll succeed!'"

He was a great mimic, a remarkable imitator of infinite accents and dialects. His reproduction of the legendary professor Chauncey Brewster

Tinker's refined intonations was perfect.[1] But I wondered why he'd found Yale dreadful, as I'd loved it.

"You write every day? Work on a schedule? That's what you have to do, none of this bunk about waiting around for the muse to strike. I always say the art of writing is the art of applying the seat of your pants to the seat of your chair. Can't just sit around talking about writing. Gave a lecture once at Columbia and I started out by asking the students 'How many of you here are *really* serious about being writers?' and they all raised their hands, and I said, 'Well then why the hell aren't you all home writing?'— and sat down. Only two ways you can learn to write. By reading and writing, and lately I'm not even so sure about the former."

He seemed to be enjoying himself and was so enthusiastic that I felt privileged to be the audience.

"Keep notes? You have to keep notes, every writer has to keep notes. I wouldn't be without old Ebenezer here."

He handed me the thick notebook. I leafed through it as he talked. Neat and orderly, the pages bore such headings as "Dutch-American Names," "French-American Names," "Mannerisms," "Peculiarities of Dress," and so forth. Flipping to "Titles," I got a little thrill when I saw such literary landmarks as *Main Street, Elmer Gantry, Dodsworth, Arrowsmith, It Can't Happen Here,* and *Babbitt,* with a line drawn through them. How many authors had such a string of bestsellers? For example, the first printing of *Elmer Gantry* was 140,000—the largest in history—and most of his big novels sold over a million copies. [2]

Joseph entered the room and set down a tray with two cups and a teapot.

"You'd probably like a drink, but I'm on the tea wagon," said Mr. Lewis. "Haven't had a drink in eight years." (Not true, I was to learn.) "I used to be a drunk, you know. Waste of time. Can't stand that two-fisted romantic-drunk-writer pose!" he snarled. For the first time, I glimpsed that omnipresent, incipient temper. "The O'Haras and the Fitzgeralds and the Hemingways! Talented men, but drunks."

He calmed himself instantly, dumped three spoonfuls of sugar into his tea, and swallowed half a cup in one gulp.

"So Marcella's your agent, eh? Tell me, how—" he hesitated

suddenly, tenderly. "How does she look? I taught her, you know—taught her everything, taught her well. I even named her! She was called Peggy before. I told her, 'That sounds like somebody's maid. You're not Peggy...You are *Marcella*!'"

Much later I would learn the details of their relationship. Rosemary Marcella Powers had been an aspiring eighteen-year-old actress with the Provincetown Players when she met the fifty-four-year-old novelist at a summer stock theater on Cape Cod. Lewis had decided to try acting and, in 1938, took a role in Eugene O'Neill's *Ah, Wilderness!* at the Wharf Theater. Lewis had always been attracted to youth and acting; Marcella was no doubt impressed by Lewis's wealth and charm. They soon became inseparable.

Marcella hadn't had an easy life. Her father had died when she was nine, her mother reduced to running a boarding house in South Orange, New Jersey. There was some talk that Lewis had "bought" Marcella through a financial arrangement with her mother. They traveled all over America together and spent a year in Duluth, Minnesota, her mother in tow, long before Nabokov wrote *Lolita*. Just a year ago Marcella had finally broken away to marry a young journalist, Michael Amrine.[3]

Lewis looked off into space. Then he snorted, "Met her husband yet? She'll leave him so quick he won't know what hit him! He won't be able to keep her mind—that agile, wonderful little mind—he won't be able to keep it interested. Then she'll come back to me. You'll see! Haven't changed a single thing in her room at Thorvale."

Anger roiled in his voice. "How can that young guy keep her happy? She'll be back! I'll take her back, any time—and she knows it. You're goddamn right she knows it, and I give that young man and their marriage one year—one goddamned year!"

Somehow that didn't seem likely, but I said nothing.

His hand shook as he lifted the teacup to his lips. He slurped it noisily and brooded in silence, until suddenly, very pleasantly, he said, "So you're working on a novel! What's it about?"

"It's a love story."

"Hell, every novel's a love story!" he growled. "What's it *about*?"

I was nervous and unsure. "Well, it's set in Spain during the war, and it's about a young diplomat who falls for his gypsy housekeeper and—"

"I'd like to see it."

"You would?" I was astonished. And terrified. The idea of a Nobel Prize-winning giant reading my little story had not occurred to me. "When would you like to have the manuscript?"

"Right away." He looked at his wristwatch. "Say, my stomach's growling. How about some dinner? We'll swing by in the car and pick up, say, the first seventy-five pages on the way to the restaurant. I'm meeting a young couple—writers. Like you! Like us!"

Writers—like us! The winner of the Nobel Prize for Literature was welcoming me into his club.

"Joseph!" Lewis barked. "We're heading out early." He slapped his knees, grabbed his hat, and strode out the front door.

When the big Buick pulled up in front of my family's sleepy shingle-style house on Santa Barbara Street, I told Mr. Lewis, "I'll just duck inside for the manuscript and tell my mother about dinner. Won't be a minute, sir."

"Now hold on, Barny," said Mr. Lewis. "Don't want to intrude, but I'd like to meet your parents."

"My parents?"

"Sure," he said breezily. "Just to meet some denizens of this fine city. Can't know a city if you don't know who lives there."

I found my mother in the kitchen arranging roses from her garden. "How did it go with Sinclair Lewis?" she asked, excitedly.

"Great. In fact, he's outside in the car and wants to meet you."

"To meet *me*? Right now? Oh, dear. Well, the show must go on." She theatrically shed her apron to reveal her customary simple skirt with cashmere sweater and pearls.

Born in Helena, Montana, my mother spent three years of her childhood in San Juan after President McKinley appointed her father, Judge William H. Hunt, the second Governor of Puerto Rico in 1901. When Judge Hunt became a federal judge in Washington, D.C., she was courted persistently by Teddy, Jr., the teenage son of President Theodore Roosevelt. Fame interested her, but didn't faze her. She loved the theater, played classical piano every day, and read avidly.

She greeted Mr. Lewis warmly at the door and invited him into the parlor. Both of them, it turned out, had been fans of the stage actress, Maude Adams, a great star in her time, now long-forgotten. As Lewis's eyes roamed our bookshelves, he divined her literary bent immediately, and seemed thrilled that she'd read many of his own books.

My father, a retired investment banker, was less impressed by "artistic types." He read little apart from O. Henry, Kipling, and the works of his best friend, Stewart Edward White, author of *The Long Rifle* and dozens of "pioneer" novels. This would be a harder sell.

"Mr. Lewis," I said. "My father's best friend was Stewart Edward White, a great friend of Jack London's in San Francisco. And you knew London, too, didn't you, Mr. Lewis?"

"I was at Yale when London came to address the political union in 1907," he replied. "Darn near made a socialist out of me!"

"I was at Yale around that time, too," said my father, who had attended for only a year (1903-4). It turned out they actually had been in the same freshman class. There was a flickering connection between the two men until it became apparent they knew no one in common. My father, who suffered from an undiagnosed neurological problem, suddenly grew quiet and looked confused. An avid horseman, he'd struck his head on a low tree branch in a riding accident years before and never really recovered. He could barely walk now, forced to shuffle along with a cane. I noticed Mr. Lewis studying him and felt embarrassed.

After saying goodbye, we walked down the steps and I heard Joseph start the engine of the waiting car.

"What's the matter with your father?" Lewis asked.

"The doctors aren't sure," I said. "He had a riding accident, a blow on the head…"

"I know what it is," said Lewis offhandedly. "Paresis."

"What's that?"

"Syphilis of the brain."

"Wow." I said, too surprised to comment. (My father's autopsy, eight years later, did not substantiate this diagnosis.)

"I had to learn a lot about medicine for *Arrowsmith*," he continued as we walked to the curb. "I should have been a doctor. Wish I'd been a doctor. I was the only male in my family not good enough to be a doctor. My father, grandfather, brother and uncle were doctors. My father thought I was a failure. Oh, I suppose my brother Claude reads my books. Parts of them, anyway. But most of my family doesn't see what all the fuss is about. They still don't think I've done a lick of work in my life."

He abruptly stopped on the sidewalk, shoved my manuscript pages under his armpit, and lit a cigarette. As he tossed the match and exhaled, his pale blue eyes squinted up at the Spanish style buildings and palm trees silhouetted in the twilight.

"Romantic little village you have here, Barny. A bit of magic in the air, and I like that. Back in my hometown of Sauk Centre, Minnesota, writers were strange ducks that belonged in a zoo." He flourished the manuscript pages I'd given him. "Your father probably thinks you're daydreaming when you sit at a typewriter, right? But you know how much blood and sweat this little sheaf of papers cost you, and so do I!"

Writers—like us!

Lewis took me to dinner at the Casa de Sevilla, an old place downtown decorated with bullfighting posters bearing the names of great toreros, some of whom I'd seen perform in the great arenas of Mexico City, Madrid, and Lima. He took little notice of his surroundings, and we were soon joined by a young couple he'd just met, Ken Millar and his wife, Margaret. Both were published mystery writers—Ken under the *nom de plume* John McDonald (later as the legendary Ross Macdonald) and Margaret Millar under her own. (They would become my life-long friends).[4]

Lewis regaled us with tales about the old days when he sold short-story plots to Jack London for five dollars apiece. He imitated London's speech and his own as a callow youth negotiating with the author of *The Call of the Wild*. He spoke casually of his ex-wife, Dorothy Thompson, imitating her reporting voice—known to all of us from the radio—expertly: "One day she came home from Washington, and I said, 'Dorothy, you should have heard Roosevelt on the radio tonight—he made the most magnificent speech!' 'I know,' she replied, 'I wrote it!' She was a grand girl. But then one day she disappeared into the NBC Building and hasn't been heard of since."

At the time I knew little about Lewis's personal life, other than he'd been married twice. After divorcing his first wife, Grace Livingstone Hegger, a pleasant social climber who was the model for Carol Kennicott in *Main Street*, Lewis met journalist Dorothy Thompson in 1927 at a press conference at the Foreign Ministry in Berlin. The next day was Dorothy's thirty-fourth birthday and she invited him to a little party. He proposed marriage to her that evening. She later wrote: "My instantaneous reaction was, God, what a lonely, unhappy, helpless man! Somebody *must* love and take care of him! And, of course, I was fascinated."[5]

Their marriage ended for a several reasons, I would later learn, but one of Lewis's complaints was that she was always working and didn't pay him enough attention. "If I ever divorce Dorothy I'll name Adolph Hitler as co-respondent," he told journalist Vincent Sheean, half-joking.[6]

After dinner, Lewis and I lingered over coffee while the Millars said goodnight and walked arm-in-arm out of the restaurant.

"How I envy them," he sighed, fumbling for a cigarette.

"Their talent?" I asked.

"Their marriage," he answered.

He was amazingly candid with someone he had just met, someone thirty-seven years his junior, and I was taken in by his matter-of-fact camaraderie.

He smoked incessantly. The moment he'd yank a cigarette out of the package it would assume a distinct character. He'd stick it in his mouth—already so bent one wondered how the thin paper stood the strain. Then he'd strike a match and keep talking without lighting the cigarette, until the match burned his fingers. He'd shake out the match and put the other end of the now soggy cigarette in his mouth. Then he'd light another match and repeat the performance.

Ashes were a problem. He'd get on a subject, and the cigarette in his skeletal fingers would get ashier and ashier and sometimes drop in his plate. That night, a ruined cup of coffee had to be exchanged.

The staff at the Casa de Sevilla knew who Lewis was, but moved about discreetly as he gesticulated with yet another cigarette and brought literary history to life with his one-man show. His vignettes transported us from the Algonquin's Round Table in New York to the drawing rooms of

London and the cafés of Paris. He talked about everyone from the old days—acquaintances from Robert Benchley and Edna St. Vincent Millay to H.L. Mencken and George Bernard Shaw. I say "acquaintances" rather than "friends" because, I was to find out, he had alienated most "friends" or had never really known what it was to have true friends.

But Lewis also spoke of the present and the future. He was excited about *Kingsblood Royal*, soon to be published by Random House. It dared to tell the story of a successful small-town banker who was ostracized when it was disclosed that he had a small amount of "Negro blood."

"Unquestionably my best book," he said. "The critics lambasted my last two—*Cass Timberlane* and *Gideon Planish*—but they can't deny me this one. Doesn't come out 'til next month, officially, but I'll smuggle you a copy." For all his bravado, I sensed he was longing for—rather than expecting—a hit.

"Maybe they were right. Maybe those other books weren't so hot," he said. "But this one! If only one of my books were to exist I would want this to be the one. Yessirree."

When the bill came, he took out his pencil and carefully checked the addition twice before paying. I found this a little odd for a multi-millionaire.

"A writer has to learn to be a tightwad," he said, as if reading my thoughts. "Otherwise, he'll find himself broke and be driven to writing junk. A writer should never be driven by creditors and deadlines. Dickens was always two jumps ahead of his creditors and often had to turn out drivel to keep their hot breath off his neck."

Lewis looked at me directly. "When your novel's a big success, Barny, don't go out and buy a Cadillac. Cadillacs are nice, but take a bus. And don't, for God's sake, get ensnared by that alluring tinsel, the long-term Hollywood contract. Hollywood is the jumping-off place, the end of everything—*fini*. Nothing that goes on between paper and typewriter in that city has any relation to writing. They buy a novel—or 'property' as they call it and think of it—because it has a certain charm or appeal. Then they assemble a crew of talentless people whose job it is to seek out that charm and eliminate it from their film." He laughed at himself. "So saying, he trundles off to Hollywood on Saturday!"

The next morning I stayed close to the phone at my parents' house, waiting for Sinclair Lewis's reaction to my manuscript. Lunchtime came and went, but he didn't call. It couldn't take that long to read just seventy-five pages! Finally at four, I mustered my courage and called him.

"Mr. Lewis, excuse me for bothering you, but have you by any chance had time to read those seventy-five pages?"

"Well, Barny," he said. "Yes, I've read them."

There was a silence. Finally I said, "And?"

"I would be inclined," he said, not unkindly, "my inclination, that is, my first reaction…would be to throw away the first seventy-two or three."

"Words?"

"Pages."

I couldn't find my voice for awhile. "Throw…away…pages?"

"Sure. Just toss 'em out."

Was this a hoax? Some form of literary hazing? "Not rewrite—rework—revise?"

"Hell," he said, conspiratorially, "let's just get rid of them!"

"But," I croaked, "why?"

"Barny," he said, "do you know what every story has in common, from *Little Miss Muffet* to *Moby-Dick?*"

I hesitated, and he boomed through the phone, *"Conflict!* Supposing the spider had been a nice little spider and hadn't frightened her? No story. Supposing instead of always trying to elude Ahab, Moby had spouted and said, 'Hey, Cap'n, flensing-time, I'm over here—come get me!' No cross-purposes, no conflict, no story. *Ennui.*"

"But I had to set the scene," I protested.

"For seventy-five goddamn pages? Look, when I want to read about the Azores, I'll buy the *National Geographic*! Set the scene in and around the conflict of the characters."

"I thought there was some fairly interesting information about—"

"Hogwash!" he interrupted. "People don't read novels for information! They read for emotion! The emotional kick comes from characters in conflict with other people or with their environment or with themselves. Sure you can feed the reader information: look at all the medicine and science I dished out in *Arrowsmith*. Plenty! But they got it by osmosis while the young doctor struggles against all sorts of adversity.

"Now, Barny, don't get discouraged. Remember, books aren't written, they're *rewritten*. You just have to start your story faster. Saki was writing a story once and a wind from an open window blew away the first five pages. He said he not only didn't miss them, it helped his story! A wind just should have blown away the first seventy-three pages of your book. There's some good stuff and promise of things to come on those last two pages. Give me seventy-five more. I'll send Joseph over to pick them up."

He abruptly hung up the telephone.

I was sunk. All those beautiful, lyrical pages I'd caressed and polished for months! As promised, Joseph did swing by that afternoon to pick up the next seventy-five pages of my novel, but I handed them over with a much-deflated ego.

At two in the morning the phone rang. Who in God's name would call at this hour? I stumbled out of bed and answered it, hoping my parents hadn't heard it.

"Hello?"

There was no salutation. Just an enthusiastic voice shouting, "Now she's moving!"

It was Sinclair Lewis. "Yessirree, at last it's going! That girl is a honey and I care what's going to happen to her and to him. You don't need to save anything in those first seventy-three pages at all! I was right!"

My heart leapt.

"Sure, there are some things that could stand improving. You gravitate toward clichés like lint to blue serge—the way anyone does the first time around. But then when you rewrite you should catch them, come up with something original. You say things like: 'The old man was wrinkled and brown as a berry.' Jesus God, that doesn't do a thing for anyone's mental picture! Why not say the old man's face was as webbed and brown and seamed as the earth on the rain-creased hills of Andalucia—that way you get a double-header—his face and his habitat. I'm not trying to write it for you, but you just can't get away with 'brown as a berry.' Lazy writing!"

All this at two in the morning.

"And of course your protagonist needs working on. Characters make your story—that and CONFLICT are the two most important things I can teach you. If you're going to be a writer you have to learn your craft. Funny, nobody would hang out a shingle before studying law or medicine or real estate or plumbing, but for some reason every sonovabitch in the world thinks he can write a novel if he 'just had time'! And without knowing what the hell they're doing. Am I right?"

"Yes, sir." Was he saying I didn't know what the hell I was doing?

"Well, I'll let you get back to bed. Say, I had a good idea today: Do you know how to play chess?"

"No, sir, not really. I mean, I'm no expert."

"How about you take some lessons," he said. "Then come east as my secretary. Forty-five dollars a week and expenses. How's that sound?"

"It sounds, uh, great, sir." At two in the morning, it actually sounded surreal. I had no idea what a personal secretary did, and I wasn't a very good typist. Chess was the least of my inadequacies.

"I'll send you the ticket before I leave for Hollywood."

I didn't get much sleep that night, wondering what my job would entail. I didn't know it then, but Sinclair Lewis would define my duties in a letter to Marcella Powers:

And thanks to you, Barnaby Conrad came to see me—an extremely nice youngster and highly talented—in fact just the sort of chap for whom I was vaguely looking as [a] secretary-fellow-loafer at Thorvale, and I have asked him to come spend the summer there, and he has accepted with fervor—he'll be along about May 15…He will really have no duties except an occasional bit of research, and he can spend all day writing and be around for a walk now and then and a little evening chess—yes, he is ardently learning it.[7]

I told my parents about Sinclair Lewis's offer, and my mother was enthusiastic and my father approved. There was nothing to keep me in Santa Barbara and I began to prepare to head East. A major chapter in my life was opening up for… *Writers—like us!*

CHAPTER TWO

FROM NEW YORK
TO WILLIAMSTOWN

Marcella Powers was more vivacious and prettier than I remembered. Or maybe it was her chic green gabardine suit and the way the *maître d'* at Sardi's deferred to her as he led us through a roomful of Manhattan theater celebrities to a quiet corner table. Though Marcella was no longer romantically involved with Sinclair Lewis, he kept her on a financial string by letting her represent the dramatic rights to *Kingsblood Royal*.

Over lunch Marcella chattered radiantly about her recent marriage to Michael Amrine and their plans for a new life.

"Children, house in the suburbs—all that corny, wonderful, normal stuff that I used to make fun of," she said.

Remembering Sinclair Lewis's passionate anger over her rejection of him, I was surprised when she read aloud from one of his recent letters:

> I send you every most affectionate, admiring and earnest hope
> for your great happiness, and my strong feeling that Mike and you
> will find it. You are a great person, both wise and amiably mad;
> to have known you has been the one distinguished event of my life
> and the one thing that will keep me going ever stronger.[8]

"Isn't that sweet?" She put the letter down. "I always loved Red," she said. "Always will. Never 'in love,' you understand—just plain love."

As we scanned the lunch menu, she asked how Red had seemed in Santa Barbara. I started to say "old" but didn't want to commit the *faux pas* of referring to their vast age-difference.

"He's pretty excited about *Kingsblood Royal*. I understand you're repping the dramatic rights."

"Yes, but it'll be a tough sell. Plays and movies about race relations aren't exactly like *Bringing Up Baby*," said Marcella. "If it sells, I know one person I'd like to see in the cast."

"Who?"

"Jane White. She'll be at the Algonquin later for drinks with George Wiswell, our friend at *Esquire*. She and her father are friends of Red. I took her up to Thorvale when I was still—that is, last summer—and she loved it."

"Jane White? Doesn't ring a bell," I said.

"She's the daughter of Walter White."

"Who's Walter White?"

"National secretary of the NAACP. Brilliant man. A friend of Red's. He more or less inspired *Kingsblood Royal*."

"How?"

"Walter White was so light-skinned, he could easily have passed for white, but he chose to live as a Negro. In fact, Red called him a 'voluntary Negro.' They've been friends for years. He's a writer, too."

The two men met, she said, in the 1920s when Lewis gave White a jacket blurb for his novel *Fire In The Flint*. White had been a leader of the "Harlem Renaissance," the flowering of African-American intelligentsia that had sprung up in the 1920s. Their family home in the fashionable Sugar Hill neighborhood had been nicknamed "The White House of Harlem" for attracting figures like Langston Hughes, Duke Ellington and Thurgood Marshall. White had arranged for Sinclair Lewis to meet black leaders and writers as preparation for writing *Kingsblood Royal*.[9]

"I think you'll like Jane," said Marcella. "I wish I could be there with you tonight, but I've got to get home to Michael. He's still a little jealous of my relationship with Red. And of people—like you and Jane—who know him."

At five o'clock I was sitting in the Algonquin Hotel's fabled lobby waiting for Jane White. Where I grew up, in Burlingame, California there were no visible black people, and I had never met a black girl socially, even—or especially—at Yale. I couldn't imagine what we'd have in common, although as a piano player I was a fan of Fats Waller and Duke Ellington.

In walked a striking woman with an indefinable chic. Unlike her father, Jane could never have "passed." She looked like a priestess from some ancient Nubian temple. I stood up, waved, and led her to a chair.

I began, awkwardly, by asking her about Sinclair Lewis and her Thorvale visit the previous summer with Marcella, but in a matter of minutes we were on to everything, from the new Museum of Modern Art building to the city's latest Shakespeare productions. Jane was amusing and natural. Having majored in sociology at Smith (where she was elected president of the student body), she was now making a go of it as an actress in New York. The legendary actor and singer Paul Robeson had helped her get her first major role in 1945—the lead in Lillian Smith's *Strange Fruit*, about a doomed interracial love affair in the South. Eleanor Roosevelt in her nationally syndicated newspaper column, "My Day," applauded Jane's acting for its "restraint and beauty."[10]

Dick Young, a Yale friend I hadn't seen in four years, appeared in the lobby, slowly approaching with a cane. His letters had described his war injuries in detail. The medics had found him legless in a foxhole in France, in a state of shock, reading the battered copy of *Walden* he kept in his pack. And now here he was with his pretty bride on his arm, his former nurse in the hospital. I stood and embraced him, keeping the tears at bay. We were joined by George Wiswell, the *Esquire* editor who had published my bullfighting articles and introduced me to Marcella to broker my stories.

After a second round of cocktails, someone said, "Where shall we have dinner?" Feigning sophistication (having been taken there once), I answered, "Where else but *21*?"

"Wonderful," said Jane with a smile.

As we all piled into a cab, a chill came over me. The 21 Club was a fancy place. I had forgotten that Jane was a Negro. Even in 1947, some hotels and clubs in the North had unspoken racial restrictions. It would be awful for Jane if there were an embarrassing scene. As a non-New Yorker, I was out of my element. Too late now—we would just have to muddle through.

When we arrived at the restaurant, I marched up to the host and waved, not too subtly, a five-dollar bill. "Table for four, please," I said imperiously. "And make it downstairs."

The man cast a baleful look over me, my five-dollar bill, and my group. "I'm sorry, sir, there is nothing available downstairs or…"

Suddenly he saw Jane. "Miss White! I'm so sorry. I didn't see you! Right this way, please."

He waved us in, and I became acquainted with my own prejudice and provinciality.

At the end of a fine evening, we all vowed to get together again.

"Say hello to Red for me," said Jane as I put her in a cab. "And tell him my father is reading *Kingsblood Royal*." Then she smiled and waved goodbye.

When my train pulled into the Pittsfield, Massachusetts station on Monday, May 19, I immediately spotted Sinclair Lewis, waving awkwardly at the end of the platform. His chauffeur, Joseph Hardrick, stood right behind him.

"Y'know, Hemingway once described someone to me as the kind of finicky bastard who always got to the railroad station an hour before he needed to," he chortled. "I didn't have the nerve to tell him that I'm the kind of a finicky bastard who gets there *two* hours before train time!"

People who knew Harry Sinclair Lewis intimately from childhood called him "Hal." People who knew him well called him "Red." People who knew him slightly called him "Sinclair." I called him "Mr. Lewis." I was excited and apprehensive, but he was in an expansive mood and put me at ease immediately.

He turned to his stolid, dignified black driver. "You remember Joseph."

"Certainly," I said, shaking his thick warm hand.

Mr. Lewis clapped him on the shoulder a little too heartily. "Joseph is without doubt the most versatile and adept human being I know. With the chimes he's sublime, with food he is an Escoffier, and he's the DiMaggio of the croquet court. But can he learn to play good chess? No, the answer must be a resounding No."

Joseph smiled. "A regrettable lack of character prevents me from making a worthy opponent for Mr. Lewis."

His employer grinned appreciatively. "Let's get home now and find out how Barny here does against the old Red Master."

I wondered if my inadequacies at chess would reveal "a regrettable lack of character" to serve as a personal secretary—or to become a real writer.

A convertible Buick sedan from the 1930s was waiting for us in the small parking lot. Now it glided through the charming old village of Williamstown and the campus of Williams College. Students lugging books, tennis rackets and golf bags crossed the street at a four-way-stop. Just a few years before, I'd been doing the same thing at Yale, before the war and the V-12 program launched me into the big bad world. As we gradually left the town, Sinclair Lewis pumped me for information about Marcella.

"Does she seem happy? Happy with that Boy Scout?"

"Yes, very," I said.

Wistful pain crossed the ruddy face. "They're always happy in the beginning," he muttered. "But you wait. Hell, if you can't be happy the first month, you're in trouble. Funny, I left my first wife when I was forty-two. Left my second when I was fifty-two. And now this ungrateful girl up and leaves me when I'm sixty-two, for one of the Rover Boys!"

He snapped out of his ire as quickly as he'd slipped into it. "And you, you punk kid, you're only twenty-five and going to be a hell of a writer, eh? Get right to work on the rewrite of that book of yours—tomorrow."

"Mr. Lewis," I asked, "just what are my duties? I'm not really qualified to be a secretary."

"Your duties," he said, "are to get up every morning at five-thirty and work on that goddamn book of yours!"

"For just that I get paid?"

"Oh, no, we'll find some other things to keep you busy. Won't we, Joseph?"

"Yes, sir," said Joseph, winking at me. I had a feeling there was more to this chauffeur than he let on. And more to my job.

Four-plus miles behind Williamstown on Oblong Road lay Thorvale Farm—770 acres of rolling fields and woodlands. As we drove up the road, Lewis proudly pointed out its highlights. It was the most beautiful estate I had ever seen, complete with a trout stream, a purposefully rustic swimming pool set in a birch glen, guest houses, barn, a tennis court, and a working farm. The regal 1917 manor house with seven bedrooms and five baths had a view of Mount Greylock, a hill that had inspired Herman Melville a century earlier.

While Joseph handled my luggage, Sinclair Lewis took me inside the house. There were bookcases everywhere, fine antiques, and four impressionist paintings by Childe Hassam. Upstairs, we passed the master bedroom and Lewis opened the door to his office. "Behold the factory," he said.

The four walls were entirely lined with books from floor to ceiling, mostly reference books. There was a sterile feeling about the room, like a doctor's office. Another desk was stacked with correspondence, bills and other "business." There was a three-way desk with a roll chair so that he could slide from his typewriter on one desk to refer to an open reference book lying on another. Orderly stacks of typed pages and yellow legal pads covered with notes lay on a third desk. Framed on the wall were two large, detailed maps of the mythical Midwestern towns of Zenith and Gopher Prairie, the locales of two of his books, marked with such labels as "Carol's house" and "Doc's place." A half-dozen photos of Marcella—some on stage, others just snapshots from their travels—hung on the wall. There was a photo of his actor son Michael and another of his elder son Wells Lewis in uniform.

Wells Lewis had been awarded a Silver Star for an act of heroism in the Sicily campaign and a Bronze Star for his secret mission behind enemy lines in France, but his death was almost a fluke. In 1944 he was riding in a jeep with Major General John Dahlquist, whom he served as aide-de-camp. Wells was wearing full officer's regalia, while Dahlquist, as was his custom, wore sloppy campaign fatigues. A German sniper, perhaps mistaking Wells for the superior officer, killed him with a single shot. In a beautiful, tragic letter to Grace Hegger Lewis, the general wrote: "I was near enough to him to catch his body as it fell. He was dead before I laid him on the ground..."[11]

I'd been warned by Marcella that Sinclair Lewis took no consolation in talk of his son's bravery, so I didn't comment on the picture. I knew several men who had been killed in the war, notably my closest childhood friend Nion "Buddy" Tucker, Jr. of San Francisco who had died at Iwo

Jima. Having been disqualified for naval service because of my knee,
broken in a bullfighting accident in Mexico, I felt deficient besides these
combat heroes. Nor could I fathom the loss of a son.

Mr. Lewis led me down the long hallway and opened the last door
upon what would be my quarters. "Marcella's room," he said. "And keep
it neat. She'll be using it again before long, you'll see."

My "writing studio" would be the little library downstairs whose
bookshelves were filled with nothing but Sinclair Lewis novels in their
many editions and foreign-language versions. There I unpacked my
typewriter and stacked my novel-in-progress, now some seventy pages
shorter.

Before dinner that evening, Mr. Lewis invited me to play chess. I'd
taken a few lessons in Santa Barbara but had shown little aptitude. Even
so, I quickly maneuvered his king into a bad position. When I returned
from a mid-game bathroom visit, I could swear a piece had been moved to
his advantage. I didn't say anything and still managed to win.

"Luck," Lewis snarled, his face livid with barely contained anger.
"Sheer luck!"

Then I remembered Marcella's admonition: "You mustn't win at
chess—not too often, anyway. *It's the most important thing in his day.*"

He seemed preoccupied at dinner, frowning over the fine leg of lamb
that Joseph had cooked and served. For a fastidious man, he had infantile
table manners, swirling his mashed potatoes, peas and meat with his fork,
blending them into a mess. After a few bites, he rang for Joseph to pick up
the half-eaten meal, now covered with a film of cigarette ash. He wolfed
down a wedge of apple pie, threw down his napkin, and issued a challenge:
"Now, my friend, we'll see how much beginner's luck was involved in
that first game!"

I followed him back to the living room and waited while he fortified
himself with several chocolates from a box of Whitman's Sampler. (There
was always a box of chocolates in every room, most of the contents ruined
for other people by Lewis's inquiring forefinger.)

He sat down at the chess table, rubbed his hands with anticipation, and
immediately set out to lure me into a Fool's Mate—to beat me in a
minimum of moves. Though it was one of the first maneuvers my

instructor had taught me to avoid, I deliberately fell into the trap and conceded the game.

"Ah-hah!" he exulted. "That will show you!" He celebrated by eating three chocolates in a row. "That's the way the Red Master vanquishes his foes!" In a euphoric state he bade me goodnight.

"Welcome to Thorvale, Barny—and see you bright and early!" he called, as he mounted the staircase, breaking wind triumphantly with every step.

CHAPTER THREE

THE SORCERER'S APPRENTICE

I was already awake when the alarm went off at five-thirty. It wasn't just the chirping of birds in the pre-dawn; I was nervous about being Sinclair Lewis's personal secretary with an undefined role, and I dreaded failure on the first day. It was still dark as I dressed and went downstairs.

Mr. Lewis was sitting at the dining room table in a faded brown bathrobe, hunched like a great heron over a cup of coffee. He wore a green eye shade like a small-town newspaper editor, and his orangey hair shot out from the sides of his head like horns. His three false front teeth were out. He pointed with a trembling finger at a thermos and a cup at the other end of the table. I sat down and poured a cup of coffee. It was quiet for a while, except for Mr. Lewis's slurping sounds and the keening of the birds outside. Smoking steadily, he stared off into space as though fascinated by a moving picture visible to his eyes alone. I finished my coffee and he still hadn't spoken. The Band-Aids on his index fingers meant he was working, for he was a hunt-and-peck typist and had sensitive fingers. The backs of his skeletal hands were foxed like an antique manuscript.

Finally he spoke. "I'm intolerable in the morning. Then I get bearable around noon, and around six o'clock I'm quite a splendid chap. You can go to work any time you want. I generally sit here for an hour telling myself what a capital fellow I am before going upstairs to the factory. Give me some more pages of your book to read."

I retrieved the next fifty pages from my study, hugging them to my chest. "Mr. Lewis, there are certain things in these pages which…"

"The pages have to speak for themselves," he interrupted, his breath smelling like photographic negatives. "Benjamin Jowett said, 'Never apologize, never explain.' The publishers don't listen or care about excuses. Give me those pages."

I worked in my studio until the breakfast chimes sounded at eight-thirty—Joseph was improvising on the six-toned instrument in the hallway.

Mr. Lewis trundled down the stairs in his loose-jointed manner, clutching my manuscript. He never merely held anything; it was always *clutched* by those long bony fingers.

"Excellent, Joseph, excellent!" he said, pleasantly. "Even better than yesterday—positively Wagnerian! Oh, if Damrosch could only hear you! We'll have to set up an audition soon." Joseph grinned at the standing joke and retreated to the kitchen.

We had breakfast on the screened porch, where Mr. Lewis smoked between bites of scrambled eggs and sausages. At meal's end, he pushed his plate aside, lit another cigarette, and showed me two pages of notes he'd made on my manuscript.

"Now, here you go again!" he said sternly. "Wandering away from the story! Don't put down one line that doesn't either advance the plot or develop the characters or help the reader to envision the scene.

"Touch! Feel! Smell! See! You should write those words down on some adhesive tape and paste them across the front of your typewriter." His trembling hands with those double-jointed wrists sketched an invisible manual typewriter. "Imagine yourself as the reader—try never to bore him. We writers are the only people who can bore people even long after we're dead. So let's try earnestly never to bore in print on purpose.

"You keep telling me that your heroine is brave; telling, *telling*!—but you never *show* me! You must *show* her doing something brave before I'll really believe it. Even if minor characters in dialogue say how brave she is, that is better, more convincing, than when you, the author, tell me. And if you have a villain in your story don't tell me he's villainous, have him come on the scene and kick a dog or break an old lady's glasses or, let's hope, some more sophisticated form of villainy. And minor characters can help bring your main characters to life."

I was trying to simultaneously keep eye contact and track the fate of his cigarette's long-clinging ash.

"Remember *The Iliad*? You never really see the beautiful Helen, over whom the Greeks and the Trojans have been fighting for ten long years, but you overhear a couple of weary soldiers talking about how they'd like to go home to their families and why the hell are they here in the first place—fighting for the possession of some silly female? And then, suddenly, Helen, in all her radiant beauty, walks by and the soldiers say, 'Wow, is she gorgeous! Where's my spear, let's get back to the fight, who cares about going home, we have to win back that woman!' Incidentally, that war, the Trojan War, is the only war in all history where both sides knew precisely what they were fighting for."

He stubbed out the cigarette on his breakfast plate and stabbed a finger at my manuscript. "And here you've written, 'His eyes crinkled as he smiled.' Jesus, God, liberate me from crinkling eyes! Sure, I suppose that's what eyes do, but it doesn't conjure up any sharp picture. How about, 'When he smiled the corners of his eyes went as wrinkled as—'"

He glanced around the table, saw the torn-open package of cigarettes, and tossed them in front of me. "'—as wrinkled as the tinfoil package of the cigarettes he smoked.' That's hardly a deathless simile, but you get the idea."

Yes, yes! I could go with that.

"You're too interested in action, Barny. *Reaction*—reaction by the characters to the action is more important."

My reaction to all this coaching? *Energized.*

After breakfast we both went back to our studies. Looking at my lackluster pages, I now saw dozens of opportunities to spice up my characters, to tweak their dialogue, and, yes, to reveal *reactions*. I pounded the typewriter until lunchtime.

The mail arrived at eleven, and Mr. Lewis came into my studio tearing open the envelopes. Most were fan letters and requests for autographs.

"Here," he said. "Play Sinclair Lewis and answer these. Say anything you like, and sign my signature to them." Then he tore open and read another letter.

"Look what this sonovabitch wants!"

He handed it to me. It was from an attorney.

Dear Lewis:

Have read some of your works and would like to ask a few favors. Please send me a list of your stories, your autograph, your picture and a letter describing your life.

How many children you have and their names.

    Thanking you, I am,

    Yours truly,

James J. Sneath

"I think I'll answer this bastard myself," said Mr. Lewis, the gleam of battle flashing in his pale eyes. "Barny, take a letter!"

I didn't know shorthand, but I managed to keep up. He dictated as though conversing with his new pen pal:

My dear Jimmy:

    There was only one thing about your letter that I didn't like. It was sort of formal. True, we have never met, and somehow I feel we are not likely to, but isn't this a democratic country? So let me call you Jim, and you call me Skinny or any other friendly name. No, Jim, I haven't got a photograph of me here, but I'll run right down and have one taken. I'm preparing a letter about my life for you, but it's been a pretty long one and a pretty bad one. That'll take me several weeks. Meantime, Jimmy, I'm interested in lawyers. Kindly send me your photo, pictures of your home, your office, a list of your assets and liabilities, average income, and the books you've read since 1930, if any. Kindly inform me whether you've ever defended a bootlegger or an author, and why. How do you get along with your wife? Kindly explain the sex part in detail.

Yours affectionately,

Sinclair Lewis

There would be many such letters over the next months. I had great fun becoming Sinclair Lewis for two hours a day, answering the fan mail—the standard requests, the admirers, the cranks, the proposals of marriage from unknown women, the pleas for money and, always, the offer of someone's life story: "I'll tell it to you; you write it; and we'll split fifty-fifty!"

He enjoyed reading my replies and would chuckle over some. "God, I write a good letter!" he'd say. Often he would correct or add to them, and I'd have to retype them, but I also learned from the exercise. Then I would sign them, imitating his signature. I got so good at the forgery that eventually he allowed me to sign his name to my own paycheck, and the bank never noticed the difference. Mr. Lewis enjoyed the deception. But the serious letters destined for fellow writers or other important people he wrote himself, and I never saw them.

CHAPTER FOUR

DAYS AT THORVALE

Every few days Mr. Lewis would send me into town with ten or fifteen pages of his novel-in-progress, *The God-Seeker*, to deposit in a vault at the local bank. At first this seemed odd, but if a fire destroyed a Sinclair Lewis manuscript it would be like burning 150,000 dollar bills, I figured.

Other than answering letters and making the bank runs, my actual duties were few. Sometimes I used a power mower to cut the vast lawns of Thorvale in the late afternoons, but I spent my free time hiking around the huge estate, fishing for trout, or sketching. As for Mr. Lewis, he napped for two hours every day after lunch. Sometimes he would send me to the public library for books or to fetch his weekend visitors at the train station.

One day when Joseph was off-duty, I drove Mr. Lewis around the countryside with his guest, John Gunther, whose *Inside Latin America* and other nonfiction books were enormously popular. "Think of my responsibility," I said, with nervous laughter. "In the front seat I've got *The New York Times*'s number one nonfiction title of the week and in the back the number one fiction title!"

"Just make sure we don't run out of gas," said Mr. Lewis.

The Thorvale guest list was impressive and the heady conversations sounded like Broadway theater bits. One weekend, curmudgeonly drama critic George Jean Nathan, co-founder with H.L. Mencken of *The American Mercury* magazine, arrived with actress Julie Haydon, his great and good companion of seventeen years. At one point, I naively asked if he and Miss Haydon were engaged.

"*Engaged?*" The way he gargled the word made it sound four-lettered. "*Engaged* to be *married,* you mean? Listen, my boy, and take heed: The concept of marriage is just as though someone were to take a liking to a particular brand of beer, and then announces to the world, 'I like this beer, it is a great beer, I shall now quit my job and go to work for the brewery!'"

After George and the pallid, ethereal Julie had left the living room, the biographer Carl Van Doren—Mr. Lewis's best friend—chuckled at my comment.

"What do you think, Red?" Carl asked. "Is George really in love with her?"

"No," said Lewis. "I think he's just a necrophiliac who's too lazy to dig."

Curtain… and set-change. Like most young people with strait-laced parents, I was amazed that older people knew anything about sex, much less joked about it.

One Sunday our featured guest at the poolside luncheon was Norman Rockwell, then America's top magazine illustrator. His *Saturday Evening Post* covers were often the sum total of an "art experience" for millions of Americans. I was thrilled to meet him. Rockwell even gave me a few pointers about the picture I was painting for the cover of my novel, which depicted the face of a beautiful gypsy woman against a shadowy street scene in Sevilla. "Glaze the background with blue and it'll recede," he suggested. (I later did it, and he was right.)

But that day by the swimming pool, Mr. Lewis was interested in entertainment, not art. Just as we sat down at the umbrella-shaded tables, he produced a handsome bow and arrow set, complete with a huge virginal target.

"A new one for Marcella—best Abercrombie & Fitch had. She hasn't come back yet to use it. But she will—mark my words! Meanwhile, I want it used and appreciated."

None of the guests expressed any interest in shooting the bow, but Mr. Lewis had paid for it and was determined to see it in action.

"Come on, Barny," he said, handing me the bow. "Let's see if you can do something with this."

Ah, the court jester. I hadn't shot an arrow since I was eleven years old at a Lake Tahoe summer camp, and the circled target seemed too pristine and professional to be ravaged by an amateur. So, as I flexed the bow, searching for something else to aim for, I spotted a huge toad basking in the sun at the far side of the swimming pool.

"See that toad?" I said, boldly.

The guests laughed at the boast's futility and kept eating their chicken. I nocked the arrow and drew the bowstring as far back as I could, trying to recall my camp counselor's coaching. When the fletching touched my cheek, I held my breath. My fingers released.

To my amazement, the arrow flew the length of the pool and struck the toad between the eyes. The poor creature gave a great "*Orkkk!*" as its legs spasmed, and died. The guests and Mr. Lewis turned to me in awe. I closed my gaping mouth, put down the bow, and shrugged as if I could do that any old time. I sat down at the table and reached for a water glass, but my hand was shaking.

Mr. Lewis's face, which had expressed admiration a moment before, suddenly went bandana red.

"Do you always have to be wantonly killing something?" he bellowed. "First bulls in Spain, then my trout, and now this poor beast!"

The guests, embarassed, fell silent.

"Well, we eat the trout..." I began, coloring.

"Isn't there enough cruelty in the world already?" he said, slamming a chicken drumstick down so hard it cracked his plate.

"Mr. Lewis, I didn't really think there was a chance in hell that—"

"Don't you think bulls and fish and frogs have feelings, too?" His face was almost purple. "Who in God's name do you think you are to kill other creatures? I guess you think you're pretty brave to have killed a poor little toad!"

"Mr. Lewis," I interrupted. "I really never thought I could hit it, but now that I did I'm not going to worry about it too much. Sir."

Taking my fate in my hands, I lifted the drumstick from his broken plate. "How about this poor little chicken? He was running around alive and happy yesterday. *Bruck, bruck, braaaawwwwk!*"

Fuming, Mr. Lewis stared first at me and then at the chicken leg, his mouth working silently. Then he pushed back his chair, spun on his heel, and stalked away from the pool, leaving the guests to murmur among themselves.

I instantly regretted my antics. Surely he's gone to fetch my final paycheck, I figured. Not knowing what to do, I stayed with the guests, making conversation and laughing nervously when someone made a joke.

While some of the guests were swimming, Mr. Lewis reappeared as though nothing had happened and sat alone on a pool chair, reading a newspaper for one nerve-wracking hour.

When he had said good-bye to the local guests (others were spending the night), he turned to me. I fully expected him to explode with anger. Instead, there was a gentle smile on his face and he said, "Barny, that was a capital idea! You're right. We've all been hypocrites!"

"What idea, sir?"

"From now on we are all vegetarians here at Thorvale," he declared. "I have just so informed Joseph. We shall be meat-free and better off for it!"

Poor Joseph, who took pride in his culinary skill, was hard pressed to come up with attractive vegetarian dishes for the rest of the weekend. It made no difference to Mr. Lewis that his houseguests did not wish to eliminate fish, meat, and eggs from their diets. They protested politely, ate their vegetables and salads submissively, and left a day early.

Over the third vegetarian breakfast, Mr. Lewis stared with disgust at the bowl of Rice Krispies that Joseph served him. He splashed on some cream, then poked his spoon about listlessly. "They're so goddamn noisy," he muttered. Then he ruminated: "You know, eggs aren't really meat."

By this time I would have given a dollar for a single egg. But I had learned how to handle Mr. Lewis in such crises.

I shook my head. "I don't know about that, sir. They sure turn into chickens. Hence they're potentially fowl, and hence flesh."

"Ah-hah!" said Mr. Lewis, "there's the key word! *Potentially*! You put your finger on it! *Potential*, yet not actual! Semantics! Very important to pay strict attention to the basic meaning of words. Now, then: Eggs don't *have* to turn into chickens, do they? Joseph! Two orders of fried eggs!"

At lunch Joseph sneaked a few sardines into the salad, which Mr. Lewis chose to ignore—though eat—them. At dinner, if one looked closely, slim strips of rare beef, looking almost identical to the julienned beets, could be detected in the chef's salad. I certainly wasn't going to point them out, and Mr. Lewis joined me in a second helping of "beets."

In the morning there were similar bits of ham in the scrambled eggs, and, when Mr. Lewis ate them with gusto, the Vegetarian Era, real or feigned, was over. He never mentioned it again, not even a week later when Joseph served him one of the nice trout I had caught in the stream.

Mr. Lewis, protean creator of characters, had no idea he was a "character" himself. And he was terribly shy about his striking appearance.

I once asked if he knew the writer Thomas Wolfe. "No," he said. A few weeks later I read *You Can't Go Home Again*, Wolfe's extremely detailed fictional account of the horrendous whiskey-drenched weeks the two men had spent in England together. Wolfe's last book was, like all his novels, patently autobiographical. "George Webber," a young novelist—what else—goes to Europe to find himself. There he meets his hero, the famous novelist "Lloyd McHarg"—a barely disguised Sinclair Lewis—and is disillusioned to discover that, for all his money and fame, McHarg is no happier than he himself is.

"Mr. Lewis I thought you said you didn't know Wolfe?" I accused him.

"I didn't," he insisted. "You couldn't know Tom any more than you could know a hurricane."

Yet Wolfe was one of many writers who described Lewis's remarkable appearance. Here's a portrait of Lloyd McHarg from *You Can't Go Home Again*:

> There was something almost terrifying in his appearance. George recognized him instantly. He had seen McHarg's pictures many times, but he now realized how beautifully unrevealing are the uses of photography. He was fantastically ugly, and to this ugliness was added a devastation of which George had never seen the equal.
>
> The first and most violent impression was his astonishing redness. Everything about him was red—hair, large protuberant ears, eyebrows, eyelids, even his bony, freckled, knuckly hands. (As George noticed the hands he understood why everyone who knew him called him "Knuckles.") Moreover, it was a most alarming redness. His face was so red that it seemed to throw off heat, and if at that moment smoke had begun to issue from his

nostrils and he had burst out in flames all over, George would hardly have been surprised.[12]

His nickname "Red" had been given many years ago for his flaming red hair, but here it seemed to refer to his scarred red face damaged by treatments for skin cancer. I believe Wolfe's harsh, unflinching description explains why Mr. Lewis evaded discussion of both Wolfe and the book.

"Now, that's the way I'd like to look," he said, holding up a copy of *Kingsblood Royal* to reveal the air-brushed author's photo. "There's a serious, fine, upstanding young author. He'll go far, that chap. Except for that sister of his—the one who runs the bordello and smokes cigars, y'know. If she has her way he'll take that position in the casket company and give up this damn foolishness. Why, only last week, the day before the mayor of the town fell from the railroad bridge...."

How he loved to spin stories out of nothing! We'd be driving down the street in Williamstown and Mr. Lewis would suddenly clutch my arm. "See that little old woman going into the drugstore? Looks like an ordinary package under her arm, doesn't it? Hah! You know what's *really* in there? Well, that's Grandma Fruitwood, and in that bag she's carrying her pet rattlesnake..." And out would pop a complete story with a beginning, middle, and end with an O. Henry-ish twist.

"Gosh, sir," I'd say, always impressed, "you should write that!"

He would laugh and shrug it off. Carl Van Doren said that storytelling was so much a part of Lewis's nature that "he could no more stop telling stories than he could stop his hair from growing."

When Mr. Lewis asked me, out of the blue, to call him "Red"—"the way all my friends do," I was flattered, but it was hard to do.

On a muggy June morning I drove into Williamstown with Red Lewis's admonition ringing in my ears: "Be sure you're back for lunch at twelve sharp!"

Browsing through Washburne's book shop, I found the novel I wanted and approached the cash register.

Behind the counter was a petite dark-haired young lady of thirty—Ida Kay, a graduate student at Williams. As we got to talking about books, movies, and Sinclair Lewis, she mentioned she'd written a review of

Kingsblood Royal for a local paper. I also noticed she wore no wedding ring. (Later I would learn she was tidying up her divorce after a childless marriage). As we chatted excitedly, I realized what a monastic life I'd been leading at Thorvale.

"You were actually a bullfighter in Spain?" she said. "How exotic!" For a change, my youthful ego was being stroked, and I basked in her attention until I glanced at my watch—only eight minutes to get back to the house before Mr. Lewis would blow his stack.

"See you tomorrow!" I blurted, dashing out the door. Ida's bright eyes and smile were still in my mind as I jumped into the parked car.

Oddly, neither of the keys fit the ignition. I tried every way to force them in, to no avail. In desperation, I released the hand brake and let the car coast down the sloping main street until I came to a garage. I explained I was in a great hurry, that something was wrong with the ignition lock, and then went to phone Joseph to tell Mr. Lewis I would be unavoidably delayed.

When I returned, a mechanic was on his back on the car floor working away on the ignition with his tools.

"Say, whose car is this anyway?" he asked.

"Sinclair Lewis's," I said.

The man stopped hammering. "This isn't Mr. Lewis's car," he said. "He drives a Buick!"

And indeed it wasn't his. In my romantic daze I had picked someone else's vehicle. God, what a mess I'd created! First, I telephoned the police to report that the missing car was in this garage. Then I apologized to the mechanic, ran back up the street, collected the right car, and sped home.

I disarmed Red's wrath by describing the lovely girl at the bookstore, Ida Kay. "You'd really like her, sir."

"Ask her to dinner tomorrow," he said, unexpectedly. "She sounds a bit like Marcella."

Ida came the following day—and for many subsequent visits—and Red was delighted with her. Unfortunately, so was I, and when I invited her to a college play or the movies, we would find Red waiting up for us, scowling like an overly protective father—or rival.

Although I was Red's favorite punching bag—and considered that part of my job—no one was immune to his sudden and frightening temper. Carl Van Doren, author of a revered biography of Benjamin Franklin, was at Thorvale almost every weekend. This gentle, distinguished historian was Red's best friend; that's what made the following incident so terrible.

There was a mathematician living in Williamstown whom Red enjoyed seeing once a week or so. Since he and Van Doren were both ornithologists by avocation, Red decided to get the two of them together, telling each man, "I have a wonderful friend I want you to meet, with whom you can really pour out your heart about these birds of yours."

He had them to dinner—just the four of us—and he was right: They got along famously. Before and during most of the meal they talked excitedly about birds—what rare beauties they'd seen, the best places to find them, the vast migrations of wildfowl, the sad plight of the ivory-billed woodpecker, and so forth. Red's stony silence was ominous, and he ate nothing. Suddenly, just before dessert, he pounded the table with his fist so hard a glass of water tipped over.

"Now listen, you two bastards," he growled, his face even redder than usual and his voice trembling. "This is my house. I invited you into it. You're eating my food. So you might have the common decency not to be completely rude to me!"

Van Doren knew Red well enough to soothe him. "You're absolutely right, Red. I'm sorry we've been so inconsiderate. Let's talk about something general."

But the party was over. The math expert went home with ruffled feathers, and even Red's apologetic phone call the next day didn't quite restore their amity. Once again, he'd managed to hurt—deliberately, it seemed—people he liked and admired. (A touching document found among his papers after his death was a partial list of the good friends he had alienated during his life. It was a very long list.)[13]

CHAPTER FIVE

BULLDOG, BULLDOG,
BOW-WOW-WOW...

June brought Red Lewis's and my Yale class reunions—his fortieth and my third—and, after a typical round of self-debate, he resolved to attend. He deliciously dreaded the affair and talked of it constantly. "God, a bunch of Babbitts showing pictures to each other of the little woman and the grandchildren!" Twice he called off the trip. But in the end he asked me to pack up a bunch of his manuscripts for the Yale Library's Lewis Collection. He looked forward to seeing "the great Tink"—Chauncey Brewster Tinker, the renowned English professor who had taken the young Lewis under his wing in 1903. I loaded our bags into the trunk of the big Buick, slipped into the driver's seat, and aimed the convertible toward New Haven.

"Damned thing is," Red admitted once we were on the road, "middle of my sophomore year I almost transferred to Harvard. But something stopped me."

In fact, as a boy in the stark prairie village of Sauk Centre, Minnesota, Harry Sinclair Lewis, then known as Hal, had dreamed of attending Harvard, but his father, Edwin J. Lewis, a doctor and strict disciplinarian, had insisted on Yale. (He thought Harvard too aristocratic.)

Young Hal's mother died in 1891 when he was six years-old, but even the arrival of a loving stepmother could not fill the pain of that loss. As a boy he had trouble making friends and retreated to the world of books. As an odd, skinny, red-headed teenager —then nicknamed "Doodle"—Lewis was plagued by loneliness and acne. In 1902 he spent a year at Oberlin Academy, a prep school for Oberlin College, where he developed a religious enthusiasm that would rise and fall throughout his life.

He was still an awkward young man when he entered Yale. Biographer

Richard Lingeman wrote: "His copper-red hair, his freckles and pustulating acne, his gangling figure, and his Sauk-centricities made him a kind of walking exclamation point—following the word *provincial*."[14]

When the poet William Butler Yeats visited Yale to give a lecture, Lewis naively asked Professor Tinker, "Say, who is this *Yeets* fellow?" The professor kindly explained, but many others had less patience for the brash Midwesterner.[15] One of his crueler classmates remarked that Lewis "was the only man at Yale who could fart out of his face."[16] Still he managed to make friends, and his writing impressed more than a few of his classmates and professors.

Lewis's earliest published works appeared in the *Yale Courant* and he became an editor and writer for the *Yale Literary Magazine*. As he saw his more fortunate classmates—the athletes and sons of capitalists—being tapped for secret societies like Skull and Bones and Scroll and Key, he developed a kinship with the underdog, or at least the *idea* of the underdog. His growing radicalism was sparked by visiting lecturer, Jack London, who drew jeers from the well-heeled Yale Union audience when he warned of an impending proletarian revolt. But Lewis connected with him as a writer, and eventually sold him twenty-seven story ideas for a total of $137.50, among them the plot to London's unfinished novel *The Assassination Bureau, Ltd.* (Only four of the stories were ever completed by London.)[17]

Lewis graduated a year late (in 1908), after taking time off to join Helicon Hall, a cooperative living experiment in Englewood, New Jersey founded by muckraker Upton Sinclair, author of *The Jungle* (1906), a fictional exposé of the meatpacking industry. (Upton Sinclair would eventually run for governor of California in 1934 as the Socialist Party candidate.) Lewis worked as Helicon Hall's janitor until he realized this idealistic cooperative was a dead-end. He returned to graduate from Yale, largely to please his father.[18]

The Buick convertible rolled through the Berkshires and cruised through the green Connecticut countryside, lush in full summer. Twice Red asked me to stop, park the car, and wait while he took a thirty-minute nap. Back on the road, we passed a dog kennel advertising Boston bull terriers for sale.

"Stop the car," he ordered. "I want to look at those dogs."

He had been considering buying a dog for some time, pondering the pluses and minuses of various breeds during our dinner conversations. (I actually knew something about dogs as my older brother had raised several litters of hunting dogs at our house in California.) So up we went to the house and met the breeder, who took us around back to inspect a kennel of yapping puppies. I was amazed to watch Red get down on his knees to have a closer look at the black-and-white puppies. A little female licked his long fingers through the kennel bars, and he smiled.

"Look at those sweet, soulful eyes, Barny," he said, with uncharacteristic sentimentality. Then he asked the breeder, "How much for her?"

"A hundred and twenty," she said.

"A hundred and twenty dollars? For that little thing?" Red huffed. "I'll have to think about it."

We thanked the woman and got back in the car. All the way to New Haven he argued mightily with himself. But Millicent Pancake, as he'd already named the dog, was very attractive, reminding him of a dog from his childhood, and he had all but decided to pick her up on the way home.

Arriving at Yale, I deposited Red at the residential college (Pierson) where he and his classmates were to bunk in the dorm rooms. I parked the Buick near the Elizabethan Club and went off with Jim Kleeman, my former roommate in Timothy Dwight College, who was still at Yale studying medicine. Over a beer at Mory's, I told him about Mr. Lewis's dog dilemma. Jim, who had raised Brittany spaniels in Ohio, offered to give Red a splendid hunting dog.

Unlike Sinclair Lewis, I was a Yale legacy and felt welcome there. My mother's father, William H. Hunt, had been a member of the Class of 1978, and was a life-long friend of fellow classmate, William "Big Bill" Taft, the future Vice-President, President, and Chief Justice.[19] After becoming a Supreme Court Justice of Montana, Hunt went on to become the second Governor of Puerto Rico.

My father, Jerothmul Bowers Barnaby Conrad, had entered Yale with the class of 1907 but was yanked out after a year by his hard-headed father, John Conrad, who sent him to the Colorado School of Mines. My grandfather Conrad had left his native Virginia as a teenager after the Civil War to become a cattle tycoon in Montana Territory in the 1870s. After his wife Mabel Barnaby divorced him in 1892 on grounds of adultery, John Conrad plunged into a gold-mining venture in The Yukon. It started well, but became a complete financial disaster; my grandfather died impoverished in Seattle in 1927.[20] Married in Washington, D.C., my parents moved to San Francisco in 1915, where I was born in 1922. My father was a mildly successful stockbroker until the Crash of 1929, when one of his partners jumped out the window of their Montgomery Street office. We weren't rich, but we weren't poor either, and my father was happy to pay for Yale. After graduation, however, I was on my own.

I loved my years in New Haven, writing short stories for the *Yale Lit* and drawing cartoons for the *Yale Record*. Our favorite pastime in Timothy Dwight College was to gather in the rooms occupied by James Buckley (later U.S. Senator from New York). Jim would mix cocktails as we waited for his pet boa constrictor Martha to catch and swallow her weekly meal—one terrified mouse. After the attack on Pearl Harbor and the bad news in Europe, we all knew the war would snatch us up. I entered the V-12 program and, with my proficiency in Spanish, was told to speed-learn Portuguese as well. By 1944 I was stationed in Spain, serving in Malága and Sevilla as a vice-consul in the diplomatic corps. Though Spain was neutral, there were plenty of German officials and spies around, and the Nazi flag flew over their consulate. I spent my time tracking suspicious Germans, stamping passports, and becoming an amateur bullfighter on the weekends.

Now at our class of '44 reunion, I discovered what had become of my classmates. Some had endured extraordinary combat in Europe or Asia, some were still on crutches, and others were no longer alive. Some were already married and working steady jobs as bankers or legal beagles. As a would-be writer I felt a bit at loose ends, but working for Sinclair Lewis gave me some cachet, and many asked, "What's he really like?"

After a weekend of camaraderie and back-slapping, I fetched the car and picked up Red Lewis on Sunday morning in front of Pierson College.

"Helluva good time it was," he said. "Some damned good fellows." Then he began listing reasons why he shouldn't have enjoyed the reunion.

"Those bastards made me feel about as welcome as feces in the punch bowl!" Nevertheless, he'd enjoyed seeing Professor Chauncey Brewster Tinker and had invited him up to Thorvale.

Years later I would read an account of Lewis's first return to Yale—his fifteenth reunion—in June of 1922, shortly after his great triumph with *Main Street*. He had mugged for the photographer with classmates, funny hats and all, and, as their most famous alumnus, they invited him to speak at the reunion dinner. After a few whiskeys he stood up and glared at his audience.

"When I was in college, you fellows didn't give a damn about me, and I'm here to say that now I don't give a damn about you." He proceeded to name the dozen individuals guilty of various slights and snubs. The men laughed good-naturedly at this amusing fellow—what a card he was![21]

But now, for his fortieth reunion, a sober Lewis had written a more tempered note, published in the fresh-off-the-press *History of the Class of 1907*, which he handed me to read:

> My chief idiocy and pleasure during these last fifteen years has been venturing into the humbler slums and ghettoes of the professional theater…going on a road tour with an extraordinarily bad play of my own; and acting or directing…As to general status, my teeth, hair, and ability to sit up after midnight are about as completely shot to hell as those of the rest of the Class…[22]

As I steered the Buick homeward to Williamstown, I mentioned Jim Kleeman's dog offer. This created a dilemma for Red: Should he put up the large sum for Millicent Pancake, the little Boston terrier he dearly wanted, or should he accept the free "unknown" dog from Jim? His Sauk Centre frugality triumphed by a slim margin, but he was self-conscious about his choice; the poor dog was doomed before it arrived.

Jim's Brittany spaniel arrived at Thorvale the next Saturday. Being away in New York that weekend, I didn't see the dog until Sunday evening when I entered through the kitchen door, greeted Joseph, and asked how the new dog was.

"Oh, it's a fine dog," said Joseph, rolling his eyes. "But…"

I found Mr. Lewis reading in the living room, the brown and white spaniel asleep nearby.

"How'd the dog turn out?" I asked.

Red kept reading, too intently. Then, slowly, deliberately, he looked up from his book and whispered, "We are going to kill that dog."

By this time I'd learned how to handle his extreme statements. "All right," I replied cheerfully, "Do you want me to do it, or shall I take it down to the vet's?"

He hadn't quite expected this response, and mumbled, "Sure, take it down to the vet's."

I casually leafed through a magazine, waiting for the dam to burst.

"See that goddamn beast?" he growled, pointing at the bewildered animal. "It barked at my luncheon guests yesterday! All through lunch! Ruined the party!"

I found the dog a good home with our house painter, and the incident was over. The black cat, William Makepeace Thackeray Shakespeare, as ornery and unaffectionate as any feline could be, continued to reign at Thorvale, mainly—or solely, I believe—because the little tyrant had belonged to Marcella.

CHAPTER SIX

KINGSBLOOD ROYAL
IN BLACK AND WHITE

Having spent most of my summers in dry California, the green grassy vales and leafy trees of Thorvale enchanted me. But the beautiful surroundings and the usually congenial atmosphere didn't help the servants or me to relax. Mr. Lewis—Red—was a Roman candle that could spout fire at any time.

I say "servants" because, besides Joseph, there was the Perkins family, a warm-hearted Black couple from New Orleans and their infant daughter, Judy, who lived in the guest cottage near the tennis court. Alma Perkins did the laundry and helped with the cooking during big weekends, while Wilson—also known as "Bill"— took care of the grounds and served as handyman. I played cards with them several times a week in their cottage, though Red seemed to resent my visiting them. It wasn't that I preferred their company to his, but because I was truly at ease with them. Also, they didn't mind if I had a drink.

Though he fancied himself the big expert on The Negro, Red had no real black friends. I knew that he'd invited Jane White and her father, Walter White, head of the NAACP, to visit Thorvale that summer, but Jane, ever busy with her acting career, was really Marcella's friend. Walter White hadn't yet written in support of *Kingsblood Royal* (which he'd partly inspired), and Carl Van Doren quietly told me that this was upsetting to Mr. Lewis.

While researching *Kingsblood Royal* in 1946, Lewis had courted several Black intellectuals like Walter White in order to gain insight into their world. Among them was Horace Cayton, Jr., a distinguished sociologist who wrote a weekly column for the *Pittsburgh Courier*, a national paper with a circulation of over 200,000, that covered what were then known as "Negro issues." Cayton's "review" of *Kingsblood* was actually an imagined conversation in a black barbershop, where a client discusses a new book about a white man named Neil Kingsblood who blithely researches the genealogy of his noble forebearers only to discover that he is descended from one Xavier Pic, a Black explorer, which made him "one-thirty-secondth Negro." The client tells the barber, "The first thing you know he lost his job in the bank, got kicked out of the swanky white clubs he belonged to, and the book ended up with a mob runnin' him out of the town, or at least out of that lily-white neighborhood he lived in…"

The barber inquires, "What did that white girl he was married with think of all this?"

And the client replies, "She didn't like it any too much I guess... But that's the thing I don't understand. She stuck by him. I wouldn't have expected one to act that way."

"That ain't what puzzles me," said the barber. By now he had reclaimed his calm and was relathering his client's face for a shave. "What gets me is why this fool Neil would go and tell everybody he was colored."

The client replies, "You see, a white man is a funny thing and he feels like he can rule the world even though he has got Negro blood."[23]

In late June, two weeks after publication of his review, Horace Cayton (then spending the summer at Yaddo, the nearby writers' colony) came to stay with us at Thorvale. Red invited him partly to thank him for his favorable treatment of *Kingsblood Royal*, and partly because he was lonely. Horace took the room down the hall from mine and stayed for two weeks. After playing chess nightly with Red for over a month, I was only too happy when Horace began to take my place at the after-dinner matches with The Red Master. Some evenings after Red retired, Horace and I would go down to Alma and Wilson Perkins's cabin for a drink.

Though Horace was twenty years older than I, we developed a collegial friendship. Little by little (and later by reading Horace's autobiography *Long Old Road*) I learned that his father, Horace Roscoe Cayton, Sr., had been the son of a slave and a white plantation owner's daughter—an unusual twist on the master-slave procreation theme. College-educated, Cayton, Sr. migrated to Seattle in 1894, where he founded the *Seattle Republican*, which for a time was the city's second largest newspaper. When Booker T. Washington came to Seattle, he stayed at the Caytons' house. There the two former slaves debated the future of Negroes in America.

Even more interesting to me was that Horace's maternal grandfather Hiram Revels, born to a free man and woman of color, became the first African-American elected to the U.S. Senate, during Reconstruction in 1870. Said Horace: "Jefferson Davis himself wrote a letter to my grandfather saying, 'I don't like the fact that Mississippi elected a Negro as senator, but if we must have a Negro, I'm glad it was you.'"[24]

With that for a background, Horace led a fascinating life. Born in Seattle in 1903, he'd grown up in an educated household, complete with a Japanese servant, a carriage and horses. An oil portrait of his famous grandfather, the Senator, hung over the fireplace. Legends of the 1898 Yukon Gold Rush still wreathed the port city and Horace was an adventurous youth. As a teenager he signed on as a mess boy for several months aboard an Alaska-bound ship, which accidentally left him behind at a remote port; stranded and destitute, he found work as a handyman in what turned out to be a whorehouse. On returning to Seattle he unwittingly helped two older black youths rob a gas station and was sent to a brutal reform school. Later he became a strike-breaking longshoreman but then joined the union. While studying at a local university, he worked for a year as a deputy sheriff in a local prison where, among other duties, he made the rounds of the red-light district, serving warrants to prostitutes.

After marrying a white woman, Horace accepted a fellowship to the University of Chicago and then taught at Tuskegee Insitute. The marriage fell apart, but he managed to become a special assistant to then Secretary of the Interior Harold Ickes. Just months before the Germans invaded France, he went to Paris to participate in a literary conference. In a three-day whirlwind he met Aldous Huxley, André Gide, and André Malraux, and was nearly seduced by Nancy Cunard, the eccentric heiress of the steamship clan. Back in Chicago, he befriended the novelist Richard Wright, married and divorced a black woman, and became involved in Chicago city politics. He then went to Washington, D.C. to work with Harold Ickes, and was soon appointed to a powerful job in the WPA. When his book, *Black Metropolis* (co-authored with St. Clair Drake) was published in 1945, it was hailed as a landmark study of urbanism and what was then called "The Negro Problem."[25]

Horace never boasted and had a gentle sense of humor. He was a great observer of human beings of all colors and persuasions. As a sociologist he had a heightened awareness of the servants at Thorvale and their identities. One warm evening after Horace and I had enjoyed a couple of drinks at Alma and Wilson's cottage, we sat by the pool and talked.

"It's an interesting little microcosm Red has created here," said Horace. "You take Alma and Wilson—light-skinned blacks from New Orleans. When she was unpacking my suitcase for me that first evening, I asked for her last name, and she made it very clear that, despite the fact we are both Negroes, that I was 'Mr. Cayton' and she was merely 'Alma,' a servant, rather than 'Mrs. Perkins.'"

He took a sip of beer. "Red likes to pretend to be democratic, but he's quite authoritarian, isn't he? The other day after lunch he said he was taking a nap and suggested I take one, too. I said I didn't feel sleepy and preferred to go for a walk. 'You'll enjoy your walk more after you take a nap,' he said. Once again I said I wasn't the least bit tired, and he practically *ordered* me to take a nap! Which I refused to do. He turned bright red and stormed off. Later he apologized, but it gave me some insight into his controlling nature. We're almost like little chess pieces to him. And Red remains the master of the board."

"Welcome to the club, Horace," I said. "He treats all his guests that way."

Horace then sized up Joseph. "He's a bit of an Uncle Tom, though a very high-class one. Probably better educated than he lets on. He's got a pretty easy job here and he does it well enough, but he knows he won't be here forever, and he's thinking ahead. You wouldn't know it, but he's only in his mid-thirties or so. He told me yesterday that Red put him in his will."

"Really?"

"That's what he said. May or may not be true. But he seems to believe it. And it gives Red yet another way to control him."[26]

I left Thorvale just before the Fourth of July to visit friends in New York. When I returned, Horace seemed glad—almost relieved—to see me.

"How were things over the holiday?" I asked.

"Strained," said Horace. "Red had Joseph make up a Fourth of July picnic for the servants in the grove of trees near the pool. It was very…uncomfortable. Joseph and Alma prepared everything—steak on the grill, tossed salad, etcetera—and then we all sat down for lunch at the picnic table. It was just plain awkward. Red kept trying to make conversation. 'We sure picked a nice day for the picnic, didn't we, Alma?' And she'd reply quietly, 'Yes, Mr. Lewis.' 'I think it's nice to get together once in a while, don't you?' 'Yes, Mr. Lewis.' It angered me in a strange way. It was almost an invasion of Alma and Wilson's privacy. They should have just been allowed to take the day off to privately celebrate with their daughter. But Red insisted on having a 'family affair.' Everyone was uncomfortable."

"I'm sorry to hear that," I said, seeing that Horace was genuinely upset by this. I wondered if he would have felt the same way if all the servants had been white, a class thing rather than a racial divide. "Did Mr. Lewis sense the awkwardness?"

"As the servants were packing things up, I walked over to the pool where Red joined me. 'It didn't come off, did it?' he asked. And I said, 'No, Red, it didn't.' Then out of nowhere he said, 'Horace, you do see why I have to have a colored mammy, don't you?' And I was stunned."

Uh-oh, I thought. "What did you say?"

"I said, 'No, I *don't* see, Red. I'm confused.' It was such a strange, condescending thing to say. Alma, for starters, is half his age and no 'mammy.' I started to get angry until I realized: This old man is lonely beyond belief. He's completely isolated himself. But because of his fear of tenderness, he needs someone he can control. And who else would better fit this fantasy than the Negro?"[27]

I was uncomfortable with the subject. I'd never discussed race relations with a Black man, much less an intellectual like Horace. Yet I trusted him. And I sympathized with his efforts to make sense of Red's idiosynchratic behavior.

Horace shook his head. "What could I say? That night I re-read *Kingsblood Royal*. And it came to me what a poor book it was. It had an improbable plot, and the characters are all stereotypes. He sentimentalized

Negroes and made villains of the middle-class whites. It was merely an attack, a diatribe against the people Red has been fighting against most of his life—the Babbitts, the citizens of Main Street."[28]

Horace wasn't the first to find *Kingsblood Royal* lacking. After the English publisher Jonathan Cape read the book, he wrote Lewis that he found the protagonist's conduct "completely unbelievable" but would publish it only if Lewis insisted. The author never replied, and it went to another firm.

Though commercially successful—eventually a best-seller to the tune of 1.5 million copies—*Kingsblood Royal* was a critical failure. When reviews arrived in the mail from a clipping service, Red would contemptuously spill them out of the envelope and feign disinterest.

"Joseph Conrad and I agreed that we might consent to measure reviews," he said haughtily, "but never to read them!" Yet read them he did—every line.

"Hell of a profession we've chosen, eh, Barny? What other job is there in the entire world where any unqualified, ignorant, talentless, jealous, stupid *sonovabitch* who wants to, has every chance to tear your work to shreds? Listen to what this boob writes!"

Many of the reviewers lauded Lewis's intentions—shedding light on the "plight of the Negro" in America—but they derided the far-fetched plot, the archaic language and the thinly-drawn characters. Nearly all said that the book fell far short of the powerful novels he had written in the past. Orville Scott of the *New York Times* wrote, "It is artificial, unconvincing, dull and melodramatic… about as subtle as a lynching bee." Then he finishing off with this: "As a novel, as a work of art, it is unworthy of the man who wrote so many fine ones."[29]

Red attributed every bad review to prejudice, ignorance, or an ulterior motive.

"What do you EXPECT a Luce publication to say!" he barked after reading a review in *Time*. "That messianic crook has been out to get me for decades! I make him nervous."

Another publication's review, set him off again: "They're notoriously anti-Negro—*naturally* they aren't going to like it. Always remember this: Abuse from certain sources is a compliment."

When the two-page clipping from the *Saturday Review* arrived, written by his longtime friend, Clifton Fadiman,[30] Red exclaimed, "Ah-hah!" and tenderly held the clipping in his trembling fingers. "Let's see what old Kip has to say! His opinion is worth all the rest put together." He read the first sentences and beamed. "Well, I'm delighted *somebody*'s glad I'm 'still alive and pitching,'" he said. "Good old Kip! And you're damned right I did a lot of research on this book."

As he read on, a scowl twisted his red face and, ignoring my presence, he started to mutter. "What?...What do you mean 'the characters don't live'? Why, they dance all over the pages!" His eyes skipped down to the next paragraph and he stuttered, "'Preposterous'? Of course *you'd* think it was preposterous, Fadiman. What the hell do *you* know about the Negro? What do you know of the way he's treated, the way he lives? What the hell do you know about life, when you get right down to it—stashed away in your ivory cocoon!"

By the time Red had finished reading the long, thoughtful review, the paper was twisted and torn. He started to crumple it up. Then, mechanically, he smoothed it out and gently placed it on the low table before him and sat there looking at it in silence. Finally, he gave a low moan-like sigh. "Maybe," he said solemnly, "maybe it isn't a very good novel...but it's the best I can do."

When he dropped his face in his hands, I quietly left the room.

CHAPTER SEVEN

THE WRITING LIFE

Red Lewis discarded Clifton Fadiman's review and never mentioned *Kingsblood Royal* within my hearing again. He appeared, at least outwardly, to recover from this most recent and devastating blow to his ego. Hy Kraft had adapted it for the stage and, for a half-commission, Marcella was pitching it to Broadway. Some twenty producers turned it down.[31] Ever resilient, Red never broke his routine—always at his typewriter before daybreak with a thermos of coffee—and I admired his discipline.

He focused all his energy on a new manuscript, *The God-Seeker*, set in the land of his youth, Minnesota. "It may be the best book I've ever written," he boasted. "It's certainly the most serious."

As a teenager attending Oberlin preparatory school before Yale, Lewis was a committed Christian; he soon rejected organized religion, but wrestled with that decision for the rest of his life. His new novel returned to the land of his youth, Minnesota. Set in the nineteenth century, *The God-Seeker* told the saga of Aaron Gadd, who first rescues runaway slaves as a boy in his native Massachusetts, then becomes a Christian missionary to the Indians of Minnesota, where he is torn between the love of two women. He works as a carpenter in the frontier boomtown of St. Paul in the years just before the Civil War, becoming a successful contractor. To be fair to the working man, he forms an in-house labor union, only to be attacked by that same union when, out of sympathy, he gives a bricklayer's job to a runaway slave. The most interesting aspect of the book was Lewis's ability to pit nearly every Christian denomination against the other. One of his characters, Black Wolf, a Sioux Indian who becomes a passionate Catholic, says, "The Protestants have no Trinity, but a four-god council consisting of Father, Son, Holy Ghost, and Satan."[32]

As Red became absorbed in his book, over the next few weeks he seemed more introspective, more introverted. I hesitate to say "more spiritual" but, one morning at breakfast, after a blistering attack on the standard concept of a heaven, he mused: "My God, supposing after they throw the last spadeful of dirt on us, we find out it's all true?"

It made me wonder, too, though I rarely went to church. Yet looking at the sparkling, speckled beauty of a rainbow trout, it was easy for me to believe that some deity, some master designer, had created this earth.

For days Red spoke of religion very knowledgeably, all the while referring to himself as an atheist. Then one Sunday he insisted we go to church in Williamstown. "I just want to see if it has improved any," he explained. Apparently it hadn't, for he slept—and snored!—through most of the service. Still, he invited the earnest minister for lunch afterward.

We sat on the screened in porch, and they argued theology. As Red got more and more excited, he smoked like an incense burner. The younger man found it difficult to work around Lewis's constant reference to "the Christ myth."

"Good Lord, what a concept Christianity's God is!" he told the shaken preacher. "Here is this supreme egotist sitting up there who fashions creatures and puts them on earth for, we are told, the sole purpose of worshipping Him, the one who created them. Then, if they do that well all their lives, He snatches them up closer to Him where they can adore Him better and recite how wonderful He and His whole family is and mouth, 'Holy, Holy, Holy' throughout all eternity!"

Red's conversation at dinner and his choice of reading matter—all research for *The God-Seeker*—seemed to reveal a pre-occupation with death. Some days we would drive for miles to visit some cemetery, particularly the oldest ones.

In late July Red asked me to drive him to Plymouth, Massachusetts— not to see the Rock, but the old Puritan graveyard, so he could prowl among the burial plots of Mayflower descendants. "My protagonist, Aaron Gadd, was descended from these people," he muttered. Whenever he found an especially interesting name or inscription on a tombstone, he scribbled it in *Ebenezer*, his notebook. We stopped by Provincetown, where in 1938 he'd first met the eighteen-year-old Marcella and begun their eight-year romance. Over a seafood lunch—which he barely touched—he said, once again, "You watch, Barny, in less than a year she'll leave that young man and be back at Thorvale." Emboldened by the thought, when we got home he dashed off a handwritten note to her on July 20th:

> From the Lobster Pot Restaurant, I saw the lights of Truro across the gently moving waters. But there was no full moon... the Wharf Theater was gone & forgotten...On our way home, after our 4-day seaside vacation, I had Barny drive through Princeton, Mass., on the mountain side (near the automobile museum!) so that I could look down into the valley...again. You are, among the seraphim, the most all-pervading.[33]

He signed it "SSS"—his secret code with Marcella, which stood for "Small-Sized Spies," a reference to their fellow cast members at summer stock, whom he once imagined gossiping about their May-December relationship. (He also dedicated *Kingsblood Royal* to "S.S.S..")

I wondered how Marcella had managed her role as mother/daughter/wife/mistress for so long. Apparently she had done a wonderful job, for Red spoke of her constantly with touching affection. And he frequently played her favorite music, Ferde Grofe's *Grand Canyon Suite*, on the record player. (He listened to a symphony on the record player every evening. He preferred Beethoven, but he would inevitably go back to Marcella's favorites.)

He always spoke well of Marcella and of his ex-wives, Gracie and Dorothy, but after his death, this unpublished poem ("Hermit on a Florence Hill") was found in his desk in Italy:

Here, strengthened by their scholarly care,

I ponder on the Heavenly sphere

Where once, most miserable of lives,

I thought of my three horrible wives.

My first wife longed for social place

She thrashed about with scarlet face

To get a chance to meet a prince.

My second made me shake and wince

By violence, by blasts and blares,

As she managed other folks' affairs,

My third was winsome, playful, kind,

But often difficult to find,

For it was hard to keep in mind

In what man's bed she now reclined...[34]

In 2002 Richard Lingeman's biography would dissect Lewis's sex life with Grace Hegger and Dorothy Thompson: Both wives cheated on him during their marriages, and Dorothy had enjoyed a torrid lesbian affair with a German sculptor and writer, Christa Winsloe, but she also slept with other men. Lewis had a couple of brief flings himself.[35]

Of course, he was never really married to his "third wife" in the poem—Marcella. Red's blind love for this young girl is hard to fathom— except that she *was* a young girl. They did have a sexual relationship—of consuming interest to him but less to her—and Lingeman says that at least one of their letters suggests they may have conceived and lost a child.[36]

Many of Red's friends did not like Marcella. At their introduction in October of 1941, H.L. Mencken found her to be "a completely hollow creature—somewhat good-looking, but apparently quite without intelligence." Still, he acknowledged Lewis's slavish devotion to her.[37] Unlike the brilliant, bombastic, somewhat masculine Dorothy Thompson, Marcella was a girly-girl, more interested in frilly dresses and fantasy than geopolitical discussions. Yet Red touted her intellect and actively promoted her professional career.

For Marcella, Red was part lover, part father and part sugar-daddy. More than twice her age, he was always afraid of losing her to a younger man (which eventually happened). Once, while sitting by the pool at Thorvale, Carl Van Doren casually spilled some literary gossip from the recent past: "Red took her out to Palm Springs and introduced her as his niece. By the end of their two-week vacation, she was every man's niece."

One of the things I loved about Red Lewis was his boyish humor. His acting days were over, but he remained a great mimic and was always full of pranks. One evening he announced that the radio actor Jean Hersholt was coming for his first visit to Thorvale that weekend. "Let's do something he'll never forget! Let's have some fun with him!"

Red asked me to create a sign that read *Paul Christian, M.D.*— the name of Hersholt's character from the popular radio series, *Dr. Christian*. He was very particular about this deception—the name had to be in gold letters on a black background to resemble a professional shingle. As I tacked it to the front door of the house, he clapped his hands together and chortled at the prank. "Wait'll they see this!"

Unfortunately, when the Hersholts arrived and saw the sign, they thought it was a remarkable coincidence at the wrong address, and drove almost five miles back to Williamstown to find a telephone! They returned to Thorvale nearly an hour late for lunch, and to Red was fuming that his joke had backfired.

He didn't really enjoy practical jokes but loved the *idea* of practical jokes. For instance, for some reason I never knew, he decided not to like Phinney Baxter, president of Williams College, though I don't believe he'd ever met him. (He often preconceived colossal hatreds which were immediately dispelled upon contact with the object of his enmity.) He enjoyed devising splendid ways he could "do in" the unsuspecting Baxter. He called his friend Rex Falls of the *Pittsfield Eagle*, starting the conversation with, "Rex, you know there is simply no truth to the fact that Phinney Baxter was found drunk in a brothel in Buffalo at seven-fifty-three this morning." He urged him to tell all his friends the story, but when Rex pretended to comply, Red urgently about-faced "for fear some damn fool would believe it."

Red Lewis's imagination was at times almost manic. Beneath the cancer-ravaged skin, ranting diatribes, and pet peeves was a man who boyishly enjoyed comedy. Once I pulled out a book from his library entitled *Hike and the Aeroplane*. On the title page was written, "To Sinclair Lewis, my altered ego, my closest friend and greatest admirer. [Signed] Tom Graham." I asked Red who the author was, and he threw back his head and laughed like a schoolboy who has pulled off a splendid prank. "Tom Graham" was a *nom de plume*, and that was Red's first published book.

Even though Red found some way to berate me daily—and sometimes I deserved it—I didn't want to leave. He was like a smoking, crackling campfire that threw painful sparks at you now and then, but you were drawn back to the warmth. He bored me only when he recited "Kubla Khan"—the only poem he knew by heart—in its entirety, with or without encouragement, happily ridiculing himself all the while. He was inordinately proud of his very limited German, which he'd studied in school and used on trips to Berlin; he would spout it to people who didn't understand a word of it. The joke pleased him and he tended to belabor it, laughing and explaining that he was "very short in this country from Bremen and could speak English *nicht gut.*"

He delighted in the Italian lessons we took twice a week. Even in Italian he made up stories. One of the characters in our traditionally dull grammar book was "*poverina Caterina*" ("The mushroom of poor Caterina is on the table," etc.). She was "*molta stupida*" and, to the consternation of our hapless little Italian teacher, Red would depart from the text and, in his bad but fluent Italian, lead *poverina Caterina* through the damnedest and most scandalous escapades. The teacher was humorless and didn't understand, so Red was always gentle with him, as he was with all gentle people. Though he often humiliated and excoriated me, he was never consciously rough with servants or young students, who were in no position to quit or challenge him. A farm girl who worked at Thorvale used to bring her pedestrian poems to him and he would patiently work with her for hours. I never saw him refuse to read a young author's manuscript.

Thanks to a friend of Ida Kay's, Williams College engaged me to speak to a largely undergraduate group about my bullfighting experience in Spain, Mexico and Peru. In 1941, Hemingway's *Death in the Afternoon* had inspired me to jump into a Mexican bullring at nineteen with my raincoat as a cape. Narrowly avoiding death—and arrest—I apprenticed with a young Mexican bullfighter, Felix Guzman, and was summarily gored in the knee. After surgery, I returned to Yale until the War came up; I tried to enlist, but they wouldn't take me; so I limped off to Spain as a diplomat and spent every weekend at the bullfights. I never met Hemingway, but my battered copy of *Death in The Afternoon* was signed by the greatest toreros in the world, including the legendary Juan Belmonte, who became my mentor and patron. Intoxicated by the spectacle, I appeared in forty-five arenas as an amateur torero—billed as *El Niño de California*—and killed over thirty bulls. For better or worse, I knew that seedy, gaudy, glorious world inside and out and had included bullfighting scenes in my novel-in-progress.

Still, this was my first lecture, and I was nervous. Ida picked me up in her convertible and took me into town for dinner at a local tavern, where I calmed my nerves by throwing back a few martinis. Then we walked to the auditorium. I was thrilled to see they had enlarged a black and white photo of me standing in front of a bullfighting poster from Málaga, where I'd performed in 1946. The seats were almost filled with a mix of students, academics, and townspeople. A college administrator briefly introduced me, and I desperately feigned calm as I stood up, cleared my throat, and walked to the podium. Under my arm I clutched my props: Two capes and a sword.

I started off shakily, trying to convey the irresistible if indefensible allure of the bullring. As I tried to make eye contact with the audience, I explained that it's not really a sport but a dangerous art, a ballet of death in which the bullfighter honors the bull, even as he kills it.

"In short, a bullfight is a ritual in which a man voluntarily risks his life to create beauty, if just for a few minutes, while…" I suddenly spotted Mr. Lewis in the audience and stumbled over my words: "…while challenging his own, uh, fear of death."

It hadn't occurred to me that my employer would attend, for he'd often expressed his abhorrence of bullfighting and of the academic community of Williamstown. Forging on, I unfurled the large yellow and magenta *capote,* and my swirling serpentine cape work drew applause—and several *olés*—from the audience. Everything went well until I explained that a bull is not overly intelligent, doesn't feel much pain. "You see, a bull's brain is very small—about the size of a baseball. In fact…."

Red Lewis's voice rang through the hall: "And just how big is a *bullfighter's* brain?"

I stood speechless for a second, then the audience broke into laughter. I had to admit he'd hit a homer with that one. After answering questions,

I wrapped up the talk, joining Ida and Red at the rear of the auditorium. On our way back to Thorvale, he surprised me by suggesting I hire a lecture agent the next time I went down to New York. Later he even presented me with an unsolicited written blurb: "This lecture is terrific—truly sensational." And I was grateful for his generosity.

In spite of his daily criticism of me—he was a master of the back-handed sting—I never stopped liking Red Lewis. A few days later, over breakfast, he handed me a leather-bound first edition copy of *Cass Timberlane*. Inside was this inscription:

To Barny Conrad,
whom a summer at Thorvale has shown
to be the most amiable man living.
Sinclair Lewis
Aug. 4, 1947

I was certainly touched by the gesture. But two hours later he was chastising me for leaving a chair askew by the swimming pool.

1. Sinclair Lewis
after winning the Nobel Prize in 1930.

2. Grace Livingstone Hegger, Lewis's wife,
c. 1912.

3. Sinclair Lewis, 1947, photo by Conrad.

4. Conrad, 1945, bullfight poster.

5. Thorvale Farm, Sinclair Lewis's 700-acre estate near Williamstown, Mass.

6. Sinclair Lewis and Marcella Powers in Oganquit, Maine.

7. Actress Jane White.

8. Walter White, head of NAACP.

9. Horace Cayton, author *Black Metropolis*.

10. Red Lewis, Dorothy Thompson, Michael Lewis, 1935.

11. Wells Lewis died in combat in France.

12. Michael Lewis became an actor.

**13. Author Carl Van Doren,
and friend of Red Lewis.**

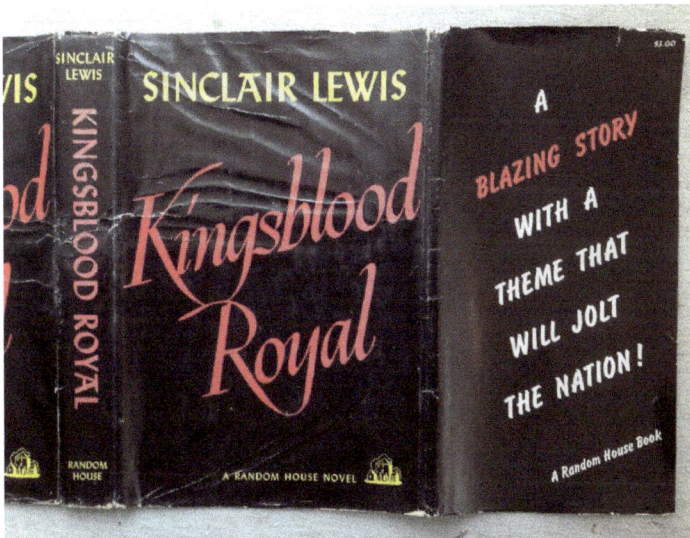

14. Kingsblood Royal received mixed reviews in 1947.

15. Conrad and Lewis on the road, 1947.

16. John Gunther with Lewis and the new dog, 1947.

17. Lewis and Ida Kay, Thorvale 1947.

18. George Jean Nathan, playwright and wit.

**19. Bennett Cerf,
mastermind at Random House.**

20. Harry Sinclair Lewis at Yale, 1907.

21. Newsman Arthur J. Stone and Lewis, 1907 Yale Reunion.

22. Chauncey Brewster Tinker at Yale, 1945.

This is to testify that Sinclair Lewis and Barnaby Conrad have agreed that all profits(including book, serial, dramatic, motion picture, and radio rights) from a story, whose plot, devised by the former is to be written by the latter, shall be divided 30% for Mr. Lewis, 70% for Mr. Conrad. The story, tentatively entitled "Thus Ever to Tyrants," deals with the supposition that J.W. Booth was not killed shortly after assassinating Lincoln, but instead escaped, migrated west, and died from a crank's bullet while impersonating Lincoln in a small town pageant.

It is agreed that the story is not to be offered for sale unless Mr. Conrad devotes at least three months preparatory study to the work and unless it be a story of at least 40,000 words.

Sinclair Lewis
SINCLAIR LEWIS

Barnaby Conrad
BARNABY CONRAD

AUGUST 9, 1947

Williamstown, mass

23. Lewis typed up the Booth book contract, August 9, 1947.

24. Claude and Red, Amsterdam, 1949.

25. Hemingway and wife Mary in Venice, circa 1949.

26. Lewis in Paris, 1925, photo by Man Ray.

27. Lewis in Italy, 1950.

28. Sinclair Lewis goes home, 1951.

29. Barnaby Conrad, 1948.

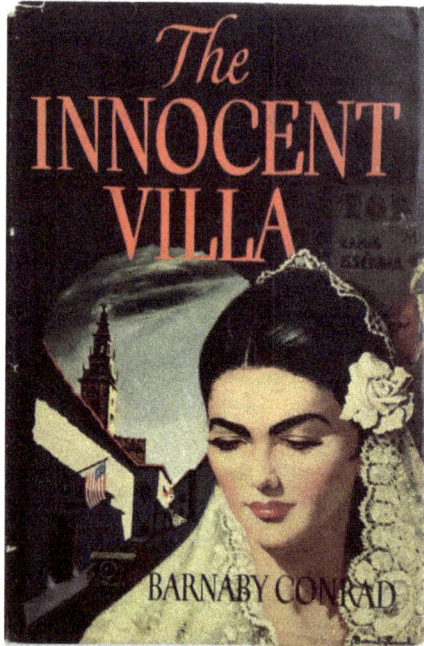

30. Conrad's first novel, 1948.

31. Manolete, circa 1947.

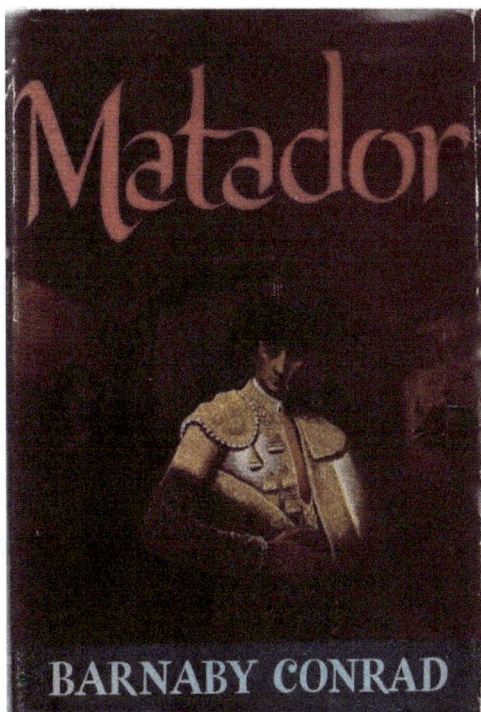

32. Matador became a 1952 bestseller.

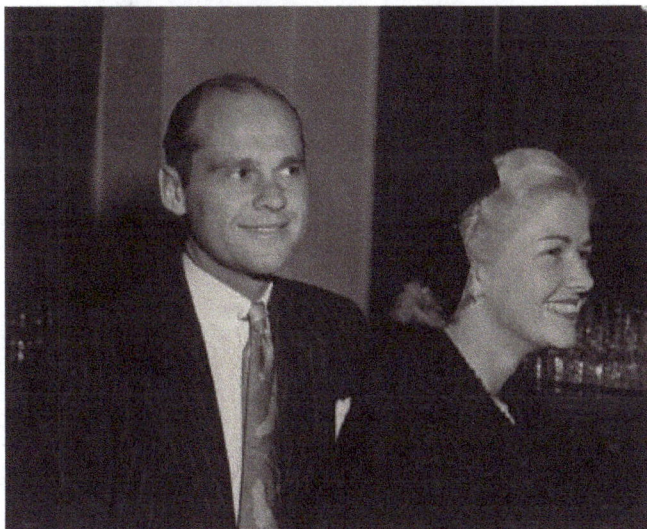

33. Barnaby and Dale at El Matador 1953.

34. Tyrone Power, BC at El Matador, 1950s.

35. Franchot Tone starred in *A Bicycle Ride to Nevada*, Cort Theater, 1963.

'Bicycle Ride To Nevada'— Kerr Review

Franchot Tone and Lois Smith in a scene from "Bicycle Ride to Nevada."

CORT THEATER
A new play in three acts and five scenes by Robert Thom, based on a novel by Barnaby Conrad, staged by Herman Shumlin, settings and lighting by Howard Bay, costumes by Edith Lutvens Bel Geddes, presented by Roger L. Stevens and Mr. Shumlin in association with Nelson Morris and Randolph Hale with the following cast:
Luchas Moreno .... Lois Smith
Winston Sawyer .... Franchot Tone
Phoebe Fletcher .... Leona Powers
Victor .... Paul McGrath

and driving his friends from him as though he were dedicated to a scorched-earth-and-sky policy, he suggests each of the strands that have come unraveled in his proud history. (I don't know that there is any central snap-lock

36. Franchot Tone, Lois Smith *A Bicycle Ride To Nevada* Cort Theater, 1963.

37. Barnaby Conrad at Sauk Centre, Minnesota, 2000.

A NOVEL

THE
SECOND
LIFE
OF JOHN
WILKES
BOOTH

BARNABY
CONRAD

38. Booth novel, 2010.

39. Barnaby Conrad and BCIII, Tecolote Book Shop, Santa Barbara, 2010.

CHAPTER EIGHT

PUBLISH OR PERISH

After a late romantic night with Ida Kay, I felt a little rocky when the alarm clock went off at five-thirty. I dressed haphazardly and trudged downstairs to find Red, hunched over the dining table wearing his green eyeshade. As I filled my cup from the thermos of coffee, Red announced, "Y'know, he really didn't die in that barn in Virginia at all."

"Who?" I asked, blinking. It was awfully early in the morning.

"John Wilkes Booth." His piercing blue eyes were fixed on a distant spot over my shoulder as if viewing his own private motion picture.

Excited, he sketched a scene: "After he shot Lincoln, he fled on horseback into the countryside. Now that Yankee soldier Boston Corbett claimed he shot Booth after they set fire to the barn near Bowling Green. But that isn't what happened. Oh no, not at all! See, when Booth first took refuge in the barn, he found a Union soldier sleeping there. Booth killed him with the man's own pistol, fearing that the soldier would turn him in for the reward. Then he switched clothes with him and fled. Then where did he go? Where would *you* go if you were Booth?"

I was caught up in his enthusiasm. "Not north, certainly."

"Exactly! They'd lynch him in the North. So he heads straight to the one man he counts on to treat him as a great hero, to give him the rewards he had risked his life for. He slips out of the barn before Boston Corbett and his men even get there and limps off directly to Robert E. Lee. 'I've come, my General!' Booth exults to Lee, 'I've come to help you rally the armies—the war's not over yet!' Lee stares at him. 'Who are you, my poor friend? The war is virtually over and we have lost.' Booth shouts, 'I am the man who killed Lincoln! Make me a general and together we can still defeat the North!'"

After imitating the flowery Southern accent of the actor, Red switched expertly to the weary tone of the defeated general: "'You—you did that?' Lee is horrified. 'You infamous madman, you've killed the best friend the South could have at this tragic time. Get out of my sight before I shoot you myself!'"

Red took a slurp of coffee and wiped his mouth on the back of his hand.

"So, in a state of disillusionment and shock, Booth reels from Lee's headquarters and starts his lonely journey west. He comes across the funeral train slowly carrying Lincoln's body to Illinois. He sees the thousands upon thousands of people weeping as they watch, and begins to understand the enormity of his crime. He somehow makes it to the Midwest and settles in a little town. He lives a recluse's life on a little farm with a girl he has taken on as a wife. He becomes stranger and stranger, brooding, gaunt, and he grows a Lincoln-esque beard.

"One day the town council comes to him and asks him to play in their annual Fourth of July pageant. They have heard his wife boast of her husband's beautiful recitation of poems, and because of his beard and gauntness they want him to play the lead part—Abraham Lincoln. At first he demurs, saying he isn't fit to play the great man, but finally he agrees. The town drunk, an unreconstructed Southerner, threatens to kill anyone who plays the part of the President, but Booth goes into the makeshift theater anyway. He is on the stage reciting 'Four score and seven years ago' when a shot rings out. Booth topples from the stage and dies, gasping, 'Sic semper tyrannis.'"[38]

In about ten minutes Red told the story almost as though he were reading it in finished form. Impressive as this was, he would make up a story as good as that one every day.

"You should write that," I said.

"I've got a better idea," he said. "*You* write it! You're almost through with your Spain novel, right? We'll write this one together."

At lunch he produced a one-page contract that he'd typed up for *Thus Ever to Tyrants*. It stipulated that "the story is not to be offered for sale unless Mr. Conrad devotes at least three months' preparatory study to the work and unless it be a story of at least 40,000 words." Red Lewis would take thirty percent of any profit, and I would get seventy. We signed in high spirits on August 9th, both of us bursting with gimmicks and touches to improve the story.

"We'll tell Bennett Cerf about it," said Red. "My publisher—he's coming up this weekend. And we'll also show him your Spain book."

I started to work on *Thus Ever to Tyrants* that afternoon. But after the first flush of enthusiasm wore off, it was heavy going. For one thing, it wasn't my story; I didn't really feel it. I also didn't know enough about Booth and that period of the Civil War to pull it off. Then, too, Red Lewis was adamant that it be novel-length—at least 40,000 words—while I saw it as just an anecdotal short story for the *Saturday Evening Post*. The next day, after writing a few pages, I put the manuscript aside and began studying the last volume of Carl Sandburg's biography of Lincoln.

Irritated by my lack of progress, Red badgered me daily about "our novel," but I still had to polish up my own novel for Bennett Cerf. I was also working on a portrait sketch of Sinclair Lewis, a side effort that did not please him.

"Never posed for a picture and am not about to start with you," he said. (Actually, he had sat for the English painter C.R.W. Nevinson in 1924.)[39] So I worked furtively, sketching him in pencil when he was too engrossed in a book to notice. I also managed to snap one good photograph of him to work from later.

When Bennett and Phyllis Cerf arrived for a weekend at Thorvale, Red Lewis welcomed his publisher and wife with a hearty hello from the front porch. Pretty and youthful, Phyllis Fraser Cerf reminded me of Ginger Rogers, so I wasn't surprised when I learned that she was Ginger's first cousin. She had been a starlet, but after marrying Bennett in 1940 and bearing their son Christopher, she became involved with publishing, wisely convincing Ted Seuss Geisel, better known as "Dr. Seuss," author of *The Cat In The Hat*, to create a publishing company with her that would became part of Random House. As for Bennett, his charm was infectious—he was so exuberant and full of jokes that he could seduce any audience.

Cerf had been a *wunderkind* of publishing. Right out of Columbia College he bought the enormously successful Modern Library, a house that produced an inexpensive edition of classic books. From there, he and

Donald Klopfer founded a new publishing house —Random House. Bennett had traveled to Paris in 1932 to meet James Joyce whose masterpiece, *Ulysses*, had been branded pornographic by the United States government. He and a wise lawyer, Morris Ernst, cooked up a scheme to bring the book to a liberating legal trial in New York so that Random House could publish it in America. They filled a copy of *Ulysses* with pasted-in letters of high literary praise from Ford Madox Ford, Ezra Pound and Edmund Wilson among others—then arranged for it to be confiscated at U.S. Customs in New York. At trial, the well-read Judge John Woolsey deemed it *not* obscene and Cerf published it to fanfare in January 1934 —with the Judge's landmark decision printed inside the book.[40]

After Red Lewis had a falling out with Alfred Harcourt, who had published all his early big-sellers, he switched to Random House. In those days books were sold with decorum, but Cerf took a different tack, marketing his books aggressively. "Everyone has a streak of pure unadulterated ham," he proclaimed. "I revel in it." Bennett had published many great authors, from Eugene O'Neill and William Saroyan to William Faulkner and W.H. Auden. But he met his match with Gertrude Stein. When Miss Stein arrived in New York City to promote her latest book, Bennett, ever the showman, wangled an NBC coast-to-coast radio interview for her with himself as M.C.

He started the live interview by saying, "Gertrude Stein, here you are on a coast-to-coast hookup. This is going to be your chance to explain to the American public what you mean by these writings of yours." He added, "I'm very proud to be your publisher, Miss Stein, but I've always told you, I don't understand very much of what you're saying."

Stein replied, "Well, I've always told you, Bennett, you're a very nice boy but you're rather stupid." Bennett shrugged it off with a laugh. Then Stein actually did explain what she was up to in her books, and they sold well.[41]

On that summer day at Thorvale, Bennett and Red got down to some shop-talk about *The God-Seeker*, which was scheduled for release the following year. But after making his bold predictions for its success, Red said, "Just to change the subject a bit…" and I became embarrassed and hopeful as he praised my Spain novel, insisting that Bennett read it over the weekend.

"Sure, whatever you say, Red," sighed Bennett. "Plenty of time for that."

The publisher then stretched out on the chaise lounge, happy and relaxed in the sun. They hadn't been there twenty minutes when their host announced, "Tennis time!"

"But, Red!" Bennett protested, "I'm beat from a long week of sales meetings. How about letting Phyllis and me unwind a bit, huh?"

"Tennis!" Red commanded. "I want to watch."

The court had been resurfaced that spring, no one had used it all summer, and Red's small-town frugality demanded full value from his investment.

Knowing it was useless to argue, Bennett and Phyllis went inside and reappeared in whites, swinging their rackets. We all followed Red across the freshly cut lawn to the court, where he sat down on the viewing bench.

"Very nice court," Bennett called out. As he and Phyllis warmed up with forehands, backhands, and a few practice serves, Red beamed. What followed was a civilized game, with Bennett feeding Phyllis's shots right back to her. The lady won her serve.

"All right," said Bennett. "Beginner's luck." Just as he was winding up for his first serve, Red slapped his knees and stood up.

"Splendid, splendid!" he said. "Come along, kids. Time for a walk in the woods."

"Walk?" Bennett froze, turned, and looked incredulously at his host. "Red, we're just starting to play!"

"Enough tennis," pronounced Red. "Walk time."

Bennett hadn't wanted to play in the first place, but now that he'd indulged his author's whim he was damned well going to play.

"All right, Red, but let me at least win a game off Phyllis."

Red acquiesced, but they played only two very quick games before following him on a walk around the estate. Bennett knew that this author, in fits of pique, had dumped publishers before.

That evening Red handed Bennett my novel manuscript. There was no mention of it for a day and a half, and Red seemed as anxious about its fate as if it were his own book. When the Cerfs came downstairs after a nap he played a recording of "The Moldau" as if to set the mood for popping the question.

"How's the book strike you, Bennett?"

"Book?" he said. "Oh, yes. Barnaby's little story. I'm enjoying it. Exciting—the bullfight." He cocked his head to the record player and said, "Ah, dear Smetana—now there's a man who knew what side his bride was bartered on!" He laughed his infectious laugh and went outside to play croquet. (The set had been purchased for Marcella.)

On Sunday, the Cerfs' last day at Thorvale, we were all sitting in the living room when Red blurted, "Well, what about it?"

"About what…?" said Bennett.

"The book—the book!" Red shouted.

"Bennett," said Phyllis. "This poor kid would like to know about his novel."

"Are you or aren't you going to publish it?" Red demanded.

It was embarrassing to me, as if my father were begging a coach to let me play with the big kids.

Bennett feigned astonishment. "Oh, *that* book! I thought I'd already told you all that I liked it."

"But is Random House going to *publish* it?" Red pressed.

"Why, naturally," Bennett grinned. "I always publish the manuscripts that I like."

"Whoopee!" hooted Red. He jumped up, shook my hand, and grasped my shoulder warmly. I still didn't quite believe what was happening. *My book would be published.* Stunned and thrilled, I was overwhelmed with gratitude for his belief in my writing.

"Let's wire Marcella!" shouted Red. "This calls for a drink! Whoopee!"

Writers—like us!

No guest was ever served a cocktail at Thorvale without asking—nay, begging—for it first. (His own gargantuan addiction temporarily curbed, Lewis would forget that many people can drink without disappearing on week-long benders, insulting friends, or wrecking whole rooms full of furniture.) Over the precedent-setting cocktail, Bennett critiqued my story and made several creative suggestions. He advised a new title, because a movie with the same title (*Christmas in July*) had already been made in 1940.

"Let's see," Red said, rattling his glass of iced tea. "What's the name of that house where your hero and the girl live?"

"La Villa Innocenta," I said.

"What about that, Bennett?" said Red. "*The Innocent Villa*. Especially since it's so *un*-innocent."

"Not bad," said Bennett.

The novel was a thinly veiled account of my years as a diplomat in Spain. Transferred to Málaga, I had a very nice house, too grandly termed "*una villa*," with a beautiful housekeeper named Chelo, with whom I fell in love. The romance ended when I returned to America after two years. I had painted that beautiful Spanish girl—the picture Norman Rockwell had critiqued—and I showed it to Bennett as a possible book cover.

"Nicely done," said Bennett. "At last—an author who won't complain about the jacket art!"

In lieu of money, I traded my book jacket art, for the complete Modern Library as payment—more than two hundred volumes, even in those days. The books arrived a week after the Cerfs left, but I didn't unpack them. The summer was coming to an end, and I had the distinct feeling I wouldn't be at Thorvale much longer.

Red Lewis, increasingly restless, took to pacing around the house like a caged cougar. He spoke constantly of going to Europe, and while he had always said, "When 'we' go to Europe," now it was "I." He needed to go to Minneapolis first, he said, to do research for *The God-Seeker*. I sensed that he had grown tired of Thorvale, tired of playing the country squire, and tired of me. Now that he had "made an author" out of me, this Pygmalion-esque project was no longer fun.

As irascible as he'd always been, his fault-finding escalated. He was compulsively fastidious and I was compulsively sloppy. If I left the lid up on the piano after playing, he would scold me—often in front of guests—growing empurpled as he ranted. When I left my tennis shorts, jockstrap, and sweaty socks on the floor of my bedroom one day he issued me a typed "room order" to clean up. He was frustrated that I had not progressed more on *Thus Ever to Tyrants*, though I was dutifully researching the Civil War for background while revising my own novel with guidance from Bennett and his editors.

"You'll never make a writer," he bellowed once. "If you don't write that Booth story you'll never make a writer!"

One of my predecessors, a young John Hersey, had been secretary for the summer of 1937, when Lewis was still married to Dorothy Thompson and living at their farm in Barnard, Vermont. John (who, years later, became a friend of mine) was similarly captivated by Lewis's humor and impressed by his disciplined writing habits. In his 1986 recollection of life with Lewis, he described the man's almost frenetic wanderlust: "Lewis flew through life. A helpless missile rocketed along by some furious inner propulsion."[42]

They parted on good terms at the end of the summer, but Hersey was surprised when Lewis gave him some unexpected career advice:

> War loomed, he said. When it came, he said, there would surely be a boom in the demand from small boys for lead soldiers. I should study the craft of their manufacture, make a pile, and *then* write my heart out. He was perfectly serious, and he even mesmerized me into going to F.A.O. Schwarz, Macy's, Gimbel's and several smaller stores to look into the lead soldier market. Try as I might to picture myself as a lead-soldier tycoon, I failed, thanked Lewis for his suggestion, and, having had a lovely summer with a vivid, brilliant, kind, driven, suffering man, I resigned.[43]

Hersey took a job at *Time*, but his own breakthrough came in 1946 when the *New Yorker* published his 31,000-word report on the effects of the atom bomb on Hiroshima. He went on to write the Pulitzer Prize-winning novel *A Bell for Adano* and many other works.

Ida Kay was our dinner guest in mid-August when Red Lewis, over dessert, asked me about the Booth book again. Had I completed my daily quota of words? When I complained that I just didn't feel like writing the next day, he flew into a fury.

"Barny! When will you learn that you write whether you feel like it or not? You'll never do anything if you wait until the mood moves you."

"But what's the use of writing two chapters if I know that they're not what I want to say and they don't come up to the writing I've done before?" I realized how adolescent I sounded even as the words flew out of my mouth.

Red's face grew redder. "No muse ever moved *me*! If I had to wait for inspiration I would never have written even one book. You young writers don't know what it is to work. You all feel that there's something privileged about your ability."

As I began to backtrack, Red grew more irate. "Just because you write one story and get it published, you think that you can sit back and wait for something else to happen. Well, it doesn't! You work for it and you sweat. You write words and pages and then you do them over again."

Just as swiftly as his temper had risen, it subsided. "A man with a regular job doesn't know how lucky he is. He works so many hours a day, gets paid for the work and, when he is done, the rest of the time is his."

Lecture finished, Red turned to Ida and said, "Guess I better shut up now before I go off on a sermon about what martyrs we writers are, eh, Ida?"[44]

Red was deep into his research on *The God-Seeker* and never broke from his morning regimen, while I worked steadily on my Spain novel. Over lunch one day he opened an envelope from his publisher and pulled out a newspaper clipping, which he read avidly.

"Aha!" he said. "Finally! I knew he would come through for me! Good old Walter White! Listen to what he says here!" He handed me a clipping from the *Chicago Daily News*—an editorial (rather than a review) about *Kingsblood Royal* by Walter White, the National Secretary of the NAACP. White stated that several people in the North had written him questioning the credibility of the Neil Kingsblood situation—whites turning on a neighbor simply because it was revealed that he was "one-thirty-second Negro." Wrote White:

Not only can it happen here, but it has already happened here. There have been lynchings as far north as Duluth in the same Minnesota as Lewis's Grand Republic....I respectfully refer you to newspaper accounts of bloody race riots, burning of fiery crosses, 'neighborhood improvement club' indignation meetings and other phenomena of white supremacy in Detroit, Long Island, Westchester County, Chicago, Philadelphia, Los Angeles, and other non-Dixie communities during the last few years…[45]

White went on to remind readers that counting back eleven generations, each of us is the product of 2,048 different human beings, making it almost impossible to identify all whose blood courses through our veins. "This reduces to almost total absurdity most argument about race." The review ended with this: "Whatever literary or structural or problematical faults 'Kingsblood Royal' may possess, it is beyond all doubt one of the most important and prophetic books of our time.'"[46]

And that seemed good enough for Red Lewis.

"Good old Walter," Red said again. "He knows what I'm talking about, 'cause he's lived it! Like to get him and Jane up here soon, but the summer's almost over."

On August 29, Red Lewis suddenly announced that he would be leaving for the Midwest in five days and closing up Thorvale. He would hire a secretary out there if he needed one.[47] My job was over.

That same day, Red and I were having a somber lunch on the porch when Joseph came up the stairs with a cablegram for me from Luis Morales in the American consulate in Málaga:

TERRIBLE NEWS. MANOLETE KILLED YESTERDAY BY MIURA. DETAILS FOLLOW.

Manolete—the greatest bullring artist of his age—was dead. I had watched him fight bulls in Spain, Mexico and Peru, and counted him as a friend. Other matadors might die, but—Manolete? It couldn't be true. He was only twenty-eight years old!

"Ohmigod," I said, in disbelief.

"What's that, Barny?"

My eyes were damp as I handed Red the telegram. He read it and frowned.

"Some bullfighting chap?" he asked.

"Yes," I said mechanically, taking the cablegram back. "Some bullfighting chap."

"And who is Miura who killed him?"

"A bull," I said.

"Saw a bullfight once," he said. "Rooted for the bull."

The New York Times carried the story on the front page, telling how Manolete had emerged from retirement to accept the challenge of the young matador Dominguín, how he'd been bested by the youngster on his first Miura bull but came back on his second to show the Linares crowd what great bullfighting was. At "the moment of truth," he had elected to kill the dangerous bull honestly instead of simply dispatching it. He ran straight at the bull, plunging the sword in to the hilt, while the bull's horn hooked his thigh, severing his femoral artery. His death plunged all of Spain into mourning.

Over the following days, I tried to make sense of it. I had watched Manolete fight at least fifty times, been with him in his dressing room, and dined with him. I now saw that he had written his own plot, his own tragic third act. I could even see a parallel between Sinclair Lewis and Manolete—tall ugly loners who had been *El Número Uno* in their fields and who didn't know how—or were unable—to step down. Manolete's story was less of a tragedy, since he had gone out at the peak of his powers, demonstrating for the last time that he was indeed the once and future king. His honor and prowess would always be a yardstick for perfection. It occurred to me that there was a great novel in this man's life.

As for the Sinclair Lewis of that twilight era, America's erstwhile "Angry Man" was clinging to a fading grandeur, afraid to admit that he could no longer craft the great novels he'd written in the Twenties.

On September 2nd, he accompanied me to the Pittsfield station. Red—I could only bring myself to call him by that undignified nickname now that I was no longer in his employ—was warm, lavish with fatherly admonitions and great predictions for *The Innocent Villa*.

"Always remember that writing is the most important thing in a writer's life. And finish that goddamned Booth novel!"

As the train pulled out of the station, I watched him standing alone on the platform, bathed in the strong morning, light like a figure in an Edward Hopper painting. I felt a great fondness and pity for this brilliant, flawed soul, America's erstwhile "Angry Man." He had taught me that writing wasn't just a romantic endeavor but a job that demanded discipline. He waved once, that long gangly arm and bony hand flailing in the late summer air, and then he was gone. The train gained speed and rolled across the green fields, heading to New York City, and the greater world beyond.

CHAPTER NINE

RETURN TO CALIFORNIA

I had roots in Santa Barbara: My father's mother and stepfather had settled there in 1914, and were buried in the cemetery overlooking the sea—gorgeous view, by the way, if you're alive. Though a San Franciscan by birth, I returned to this charming coastal town because of its Mission-style architecture and its village-like aspect, but also because I enjoyed the luxury of free room and board at my parents' house. The perks of bourgeois bohemia.

I didn't look up many of my old friends, but I did track down a friend of Red Lewis—the legendary British poet, Alfred Noyes, author of the classic 1906 poem, "The Highwayman"—which we all memorized in grammar school. I often swam in the ocean with him and his family, and though he was almost seventy, he bravely paddled way out beyond the breakers. Nearly blind from glaucoma, he would say, "Dear boy, do keep an eye on me. If I lose m'direction, get twisted about, I might veddy easily end up on Catalina Island!"

For the most part, I lived a quiet life, as I rewrote *The Innocent Villa* and, with less enthusiasm, researched the Booth novel. I received several letters from Red Lewis, some warm and encouraging, others cold and cutting, depending upon his mood. Occasionally he asked for news of Marcella. In October I sent him a note about my research for our John Wilkes Booth book, telling him that I'd discovered that as a boy the assassin had tattooed his initials JWB on his wrist. Red Lewis wrote me from the St. Paul Hotel in Minnesota:

Your letter sounds as tho you were doing just the right work on So Ever research. I'm delighted. With JWB on his wrist, he might become either Jago (=Iago) or Jackson (for Stonewall) Boyd.

My trip was wonderful... & now I'm settled here couple months, working in fine State Historical Society's fine MS collection. And missing Thorvale! And chess! Write me.[48]

On November 30, he wrote from Thorvale after finishing his research for *The God-Seeker* in Minnesota:

Dear Barny,

I'm a little concerned about your dropping Booth. I can't be sure, but I rather think that unless you do it now, you never will, and your invisible psychological chart will show, permanently, a curve of defeat.[49]

His letter puzzled me. Why did this Booth novel mean so much to him? Why was it so important that I write a historical novel about a man most Americans despised? I had my own life to live. I resented his schoolmarm-ish scolding, and yet I owed him much for the summer at Thorvale.... and I missed him. *Writers—like us.*

In the same letter he announced: "After much meditation on the Bishops and the futility of ever expecting them to make the farm anything like pay, I have suddenly shut down all the farming operations excepting keeping three cows and a few chickens just for ourselves, to be cared for by Bill Perkins."

He went on to say that the farmer, Charley Bishop, was "bewildered" by his decision, but that "I'll save several hundred dollars a month—and eliminate the constant mild ill-feeling between my Negro colony and those superior white folks at the foot of the hill."[50]

I had never noticed any "ill-feeling" between his "Negro colony" and the "superior white folks" who had always struck me as nice, simple farmers. And what would Horace Cayton have made of this paternalistic comment? I would later learn that the Bishops, who had known no life other than farming, were thus forced into great hardship after being cast out—but in theory it saved Red some money.

Another scolding letter from Red Lewis merely said:

I take it that, this winter, you have decided that you are not going to be a writer–not at all. Your decision, or at least hankering, to flee off to the bogus paradises of Paris and Naples after a winter devoted to aimless idleness, is the old story. That your decision is unconscious probably makes it only the more final."[51]

The cold rebuke of this letter was softened somewhat by an upbeat letter from Ida Kay, now acting as Thorvale's house manager while Red was in the Midwest:

But Barnaby it would warm your heart—never does he get away from the subject of you, your writing and your book! He attacks you mercilessly, then immediately comes to your rescue before he beats you to a pulp. He criticizes you severely and then immediately praises you to the skies... I have yet to be up there for one evening, but at least one half hour is spent on a certain, former secretary, his faults, his virtues, his many and varied abilities, his destiny, his failings, his writing career or lack of one....[52]

Ida's words made me nostalgic for my summer at Thorvale; but it also goaded me to prove I had what it took to be a writer. Meanwhile, I'd finished the revisions on *The Innocent Villa*. As publication day approached, I felt even more like an author when Random House scheduled book-signing parties for me in Santa Barbara and San Francisco.

Then a letter from Sinclair Lewis arrived:

The book has come, handsomely autographed, and it looks extremely good—including your jacket picture...You're probably right in saying that I am too hard on you as an active conscientious objector to writing—I am likely to go on being so because of your peculiar peril of being highly versatile and talented—two of the worst crosses any young writer can bear.

I am doing nothing whatever but work—though I suppose that I must, without noticing it, occasionally sleep and eat.[53]

It was now 1948, and Red was most likely finalizing the manuscript of *The God-Seeker*, which would appear in 1949. He had made hundreds of pages of notes before even starting it; Mark Schorer would later comment mordantly, "He had probably never worked so hard, certainly never to such little point." The book came out to lukewarm reviews—none overly bruising—but it barely sold 30,000 copies, a disaster for a book by Sinclair Lewis.

As reviews of *The Innocent Villa* appeared I soon understood how Red had felt when battered by critics. My first blow came from *The New Yorker*. After a brief and routine summary of my plot, the paragraph concluded: "According to his publishers, Mr. Conrad once overcame a bull in a Spanish ring himself and was awarded his opponent's ears by the crowd for his trouble. He is hardly in a position to be granted a comparable tribute by the readers of his first novel."[54]

Marcella was quick to soothe my bleats of pain. She forwarded two favorable clippings: One from the *Washington Star* and another from the *Cleveland News* which concluded, "the author deserves both ears for this exciting effort."

Then came a lengthy critique from the *Brooklyn Daily Eagle* arrived. One Professor F. Cordasco wrote: "Out of the limbo of lost novelists has come Barnaby Conrad whose *The Innocent Villa* is his passport to literary perdition." After that comparatively laudatory beginning, the good professor then rolled up his sleeves, broke out the scalpel, and began slicing apart my characters: "Puppets…shabby…patently false…irritating…sad tribute to the Consular Service of the United States."

It seemed perfectly rational for me to scream at the clipping, "What do you mean phony characters, Cordasco? They were real people. I *knew* those people because I lived with them. What the hell do you know about Spain, you damned Italian pedant!" As I bellowed at the scrap of paper, I thought, *Good God, Conrad, you're becoming Sinclair Lewis!* At least Red had written many good books before his downturn.

Cordasco's review ended with this indictment: "The publishers tell us that Mr. Conrad was conceded the ears of the dead bull for one of his performances in the ring…for this novel Mr. Conrad will be conceded only the ugly cries of an obstetrical monstrosity that should never have seen the light."[55]

Writers—like us!

Years later, novelist Herb Gold told me with mock envy, "Oh, to have written a book which could inspire such a review!" But at the time, I couldn't be objective about the attack.

Marcella sent me a soothing *New York Times* review in which Charles Poore first identified the plot as "a treatment, shall we say, of the Madam Butterfly theme…," then went on: "His hero, Lance Peters, is a strayed reveler from the American coteries that used to breeze happily through Pamplona and Madrid with copies of *The Sun Also Rises* under their arms and an interest in bullfights and manzanilla… complete with a last-minute troublesome love affair. If you don't take it all too seriously, you can have quite a lot of fun out of the book."[56]

But after the first flush of authorhood, the inevitable let-down arrived. Magazines weren't buying either my fiction or my articles, and I had no burning plot ideas for another novel. At times I wondered if Sinclair Lewis had been right: I would never write another book; I simply was not a writer.

"The world is filled with one-book authors," Lewis had sneered once. *Writers—like us!* Welcome to the club.

My older brother Hunt, who had been working in the import-export business in Lima, returned to San Francisco and invited me to share a bachelor pad on Telegraph Hill, a quaint shingled cottage with floors sloped like those of a mystery house.

Purposeless, I began hanging around a nondescript bar called Twelve Adler Place, on Columbus near the Old Barbary Coast district. Other writers and *artistes manqués* frequented the joint, because the drinks were cheap.

I didn't have a dime. I was selling my blood to a blood bank as often as possible for four dollars a shot. I was about to take a busboy job in a cafeteria for seven dollars a day plus meals. On my way out the door to report for my first day of work, the mailman handed me a letter from Marcella. The short story I'd written months before ("Cayetano the Perfect") had been accepted by *Collier's* for $750—a fortune in those days. Buoyed by the magazine sale, I returned to the typewriter. A week later, Marcella wired me that "Cayetano" had also won the Collier's Story prize—for an additional $1000. (It subsequently was included in the 1949 O. Henry Prize Stories collection.)

The next round of setbacks, however, made me question the writer's life. I was achieving neither fame, nor fortune, nor steady income. While my contemporaries were all progressing in their "real" careers as lawyers, doctors or businessmen, and getting married, I was still a bachelor with no secure professional path. *Writers, like us.*

Then I spotted Dale Cowgill at the wedding party of friends in Burlingame, where we had both lived as children. At twenty-two she was petite and demure, her blond beauty reminiscent of Prince Valiant's wife, Aleta. Though four years my junior, Dale had attended my grade school and her parents knew mine. She had just graduated pre-med from Stanford and was doing research for her own edification. I invited her to dinner that night, but she said she had reading to do, so I escorted her to her car. On the front seat of her beat-up Chevy lay copies of *Coming of Age in Samoa*, *Calculus is Fun!*, *The Life of Freud* and *Scientific American*. Intrigued, I called her the next morning. On our first date I took her to the Opera House for *La Bohème*. She loved the opera and I was enchanted by her understated braininess and easy laugh.

A day later, Dale called to say there was an opening for a columnist on the Women's Page of the *San Francisco News*—would I help her write some sample columns? We spent a week collecting items and writing them up in front of the fire in my little cottage overlooking the Bay, serenaded by the foghorns. Our efforts to make the writing sprightly and informative succeeded; Dale was awarded the social column "Buttons and Bows" the following week. After that, we saw each other every day, and life took on a brighter glow.

CHAPTER TEN

AMERICANS ABROAD

In October of 1948, while I was courting Dale in San Francisco, Sinclair Lewis wrapped up *The God-Seeker*, put Thorvale on the market, and prepared for a six-month sojourn in Europe.

Red spent his last night ashore with Bennett and Phyllis Cerf at their Manhattan townhouse. A friend, Bob Haas, telephoned Bennett to say that William Faulkner was in town and asked if the Cerfs would like to join them. Bennett relayed the information to his houseguest.

"No!" said Red, vehemently. "This is *my* night, Bennett. Haven't you been a publisher long enough to understand I don't want to share it with another author?"

Bennett diplomatically declined the invitation and amiably entertained his guest until Red, mentioning an early morning departure, retired upstairs to the guest room.

It was still early, and Bennett and Phyllis were nursing drinks in the living room when Red shouted down the stairwell.

"Bennett! Bennett!"

Alarmed, Bennett rushed up the stairs. "Red? What is it?"

Lewis smiled. "Just wanted to be sure you hadn't slipped out to see Faulkner. Goodnight."[57]

On the morning of October 19th, Joseph Hardrick drove Red and Katherine Powers, Marcella's mother, to the S.S. *Saturnia*. He had originally invited Carl Van Doren to come to Europe with him, but his old friend had just undergone eye surgery and begged off. So Red fell back on Mrs. Powers for her easy if dull companionship—and to stay connected with Marcella.

While Joseph supervised the transfer of a huge pile of luggage from the car to their staterooms, Lewis granted reporters a shipboard interview, and predicted the election victory of Thomas Dewey over Harry Truman in November. Joseph waved goodbye to his employer at the gangway and drove off to Williamstown.

After a few hours at sea, it appeared that two of Mrs. Powers's suitcases were missing. Lewis became furious and began to catalogue Joseph's various shortcomings over the years. Even though the misplaced bags eventually turned up on board, when Lewis reached Rome he fired Hardrick by telegram. And that's how this faithful old employee was cut out of his will and left without a pension.

Lewis must have felt some guilt over this action, some need to justify it, because months later, he wrote from the Hotel Excelsior in Florence to Ida Kay, who was still keeping an eye on Thorvale:

> After absence and earnestly thinking about it, I have fired Joseph—he is to be gone-the-hell-out-of-there before I get back. This is final and don't waste your time or encourage him by pleading for him. He had become so bored by his job that he was criminally slighting it, and he is incurable. My fault—I realize here, with this beautiful food, that I should never have let him get away with the miserable tastelessnesses out of cans that, more and more, in a few minutes daily which he condescended to devote to cooking, he slapped out. (St. Cloud Archives)[58]

Lewis settled into life in Florence, where he was often entertained by Bernard Berenson at his fabled *Villa I Tatti*. As he hobnobbed with the Anglo-American community, he wrote to Ida Kay:

> It's an enchanted colony in an enchanted town and the king of it all is B.B.—Bernard Berenson—, the gtest [sic] authority on Italian cinquecento art—but I doubt if I'd ever work here, and so much of the horrid New England puritanism I do have: I feel guilty without work.[59]

Berenson had heard rumors of Lewis's strange looks and behavior, but was impressed by "his fine blue eyes," his fastidious dress, and his cheerful demeanor. Though Lewis knew little about painting, the two men amused each other with word games that Red had once played with his

Yale professor, Chauncey Brewster Tinker.[60]

Two weeks later Red wrote Ida again:

Mrs. Powers is amazingly happy here; loves crooked streets and
old towers and the excellent restaurants…Next week she goes
down to Rome by herself for an audience with the Pope! We tell
her that she will come back a holy woman and no longer touch
wine, cigarettes and the jazz which, on the radio, we get from
Rome, Madrid, and the American Forces in Germany.[61]

Lewis became so fond of The Reverend Sturges Riddle, the young
rector at St. James American Episcopal Church, and his fashionable wife,
that he wrote: "This couple, blast them, are so charming that all of us—
atheists, Jews, shouting Methodists, fishblooded Congregationalists, go
meekly to his church every Sunday morning…and have cocktails with him
later in the week!"[62]

And there were others for Lewis to alternately charm or offend. He
had lunch with Harold Acton and Evelyn Waugh and castigated Edith and
Osbert Sitwell for their British snobbery towards Americans, then waxed
elegiac over the beauty of the Minnesota prairies. "I love America," he
would say. "but I don't like it."[63]

After a month in Florence, Lewis grew restless. With car and driver,
he and Mrs. Powers toured the churches and museums of the northern
Italian cities until mid-March, 1949, when they reached Venice and
checked into the magnificent Gritti Palace Hotel. There he kept up his
daily regimen of writing four hours a day—working on a new novel, *Over
the Body of Lucy Jade.*

Ernest Hemingway and his fourth wife Mary Welsh, a native of Red's
Minnesota, were also staying at the Gritti Palace. Though both
Hemingway and Lewis had been in Paris in 1922, and had said kind and
unkind things about each other in print, they didn't actually meet until
1927, when they met in Berlin. Then, in 1940, Lewis made a short trip to
Cuba, where Hemingway and his previous wife, Martha Gellhorn,
welcomed Lewis and the very young Marcella Powers to the Finca Vigía.
Hemingway had pointedly served a plate of roasted woodcock, with beak
and feet intact, to tweak the finicky older author. Now, from Venice,

Hemingway would write to his publisher Charles Scribner that Lewis was here "liveing [sic] with the mother of his ex-mistress Marcella Powers." Papa felt compelled to belittle Mrs. Powers's and Red's provincial curiosity about the Old World:

> The mother very neat and well washed and always calling him Mister Lewis. They had the regal suite at the Gritti. He would go down to the bar and have three or four double whiskies in the evening and then write. Sometimes he would write in the mornings too. But mostly at night. The rest of the time he would go with Mrs. Powers and peer at whatever was 3 starred in Baedeker.[64]

Red Lewis was drinking again, and that made him more critical and combative. One day while Hemingway was out of the hotel, Lewis took it upon himself to warn Mary about the difficulties of being married to a writer. In his know-it-all way, he declared that Ernest should be bringing out a novel every year.

Later Mary described Lewis in a letter: "His face was a piece of old liver, shot squarely with a #7 shot at twenty yards. His hands trembled when he ate, blobs of everything oozing out between his lips." And then, with a tiny bit of kindness, she added, "His mind was still sharp and glib and slick and I could accept him because he loved Italy."[65]

Then Lewis berated Hemingway face-to-face for never writing positively about his books after he had been so kind to Papa's novels—even championing him back in 1930 as a future candidate for the Nobel Prize. After this earful, Hemingway wrote to Scribner: "How the hell could I write about his books. Only kind thing is silence."[66]

Both men were competitive, but Hemingway had a cruel streak. He did a nasty job on Lewis's physical appearance in his next novel, *Across the River and Into the Trees*, where Colonel Cantwell, sitting in Harry's Bar in Venice, observes "the writer":

> They looked at the man at the third table. He had a strange face—like an over-enlarged, disappointed weasel or ferret. It looked as pock-marked and as blemished as the mountains of the moon seen through a cheap telescope and, the Colonel thought, it looked like

Goebbels' face, if Goebbels had ever been in a plane that burned and not been able to get out before the fire reached him..."[67]

This harsh vignette appeared in one of Hemingway's worst books, his first novel in ten years. It begins with masterful chapters on duck-hunting in Venice, but dissolves into an embarassing self-parody. Although he would win the Nobel Prize three years later, Hemingway was on the downslide himself, plagued—like Lewis—by skin disease and the alcoholism that scarred his liver and brain.

Red Lewis and I were still in touch by letter, and that winter I proudly sent him a romantic snapshot of my fiancée, gushing about Dale's many attributes. I also told him that after our spring wedding we'd be touring Europe as roaming journalists.

In March 1949, Red wrote to me from the Albergo Windsor Savoia in Assisi:

Dear Barny,

Despite all apostolic warnings about marriage and newspaper work, I highly approve of Your Girl, both from your account of her and from her picture (and don't let her say, "What the hell right has <u>he</u> to approve or disapprove!" tho that would be natural). And of your dual wandering job. It would be pleasant if I could encounter you on the way, though my plans are not precise enough for me to give adequate addresses. I'll be in Venice early in April, for a week or two, then on Lake Como, in Milan, and about Genoa. You could enquire! My most fervent wishes for the happiness of both of you. Ever, Red[68]

On March 19, 1949, Dale and I were married at her family's grand Tudor house in Burlingame, California. As a wedding present, my father-in-law gave us the princely sum of $5,000, saying, "Don't come back from your honeymoon until it's all spent."

We took a train to New York and on April 1ˢᵗ boarded the *S.S. Sobieski*, and sailed to Spain. There we spent six weeks at the sprawling old Hotel Santa Clara in Torremolinas, first as guests, then as impromptu managers while the owners went off on their own vacation. In the musty bar of the hotel was an upright piano with a single sheet of sheet music on it: "Dream of Olwyn," a haunting song I loved and played for the rest of my life. We watched many bullfights in Sevilla, then sailed to Morocco where poor Dale got sick from the food.

Dale was now writing a "A Cook's Tour," for the *San Francisco News,* a weekly column about the various restaurants and recipes we encountered in our travels. In Rome we wandered through its ancient ruins, which I sketched. During an audience with the Pope a cardinal asked Dale if she had a question for His Holiness; she said, "Yes: What is his favorite recipe?" The startled cleric replied, "I'm sorry, *signora*, His Holiness does not answer such questions."

After visiting every museum in Florence, in July we stayed in a nice flat in the Rue de Verneuil on Paris's Left Bank. The owner was the Countess von Wurmbrand, mother of an American friend in San Francisco. Paris was on the mend after the War. On a wall near our building's entrance was a plaque commemorating the Resistance fighters who had been executed by the Germans; you could still see bullet holes in the wall. Every few days a bouquet of flowers was left on the sidewalk in their memory.

The ghosts of 1920s American expatriates still hovered in the Left Bank cafés. Hemingway had not yet published his great memoir, *A Moveable Feast*, but I knew that he and Fitzgerald had frequented the Deux Magots, Le Dôme, and Le Select, where we sometimes enjoyed an *apéritif* on the terrace. At the Café Flore I spotted the pipe-smoking existentialist Jean-Paul Sartre with Simone de Beauvoir, but I barely knew who they were.

One afternoon, at the large Fourth of July party at the American Embassy, Dale spotted a schoolmate from St. Timothy's School, Lee Fahnestock, who was on her honeymoon with John ("Jack") Leggett, who had graduated from Yale a few years ahead of me. Both were literary, spoke good French, and took an interest in painting and writing. The Leggetts had arrived in Paris with a letter of introduction to Alice B. Toklas, the life-companion of the late Gertrude Stein. They had already taken tea with Miss Toklas at their famed modernist salon in the rue Fleurus. "The paintings by Matisse and Picasso were fabulous," said Lee, "but her dog Basket had very bad breath."

As our landlord had given us the use of a car, Dale and I invited the Leggetts to explore the French countryside. At one point in our wandering road trip, Jack and I happily recited in unison the first eighteen lines of Chaucer's *Canterbury Tales*, which was once a required memory skill for all Yale graduates. Our brides were not impressed, but it was a jolly trip. We headed out to Normandy and Brittany for a week, visiting the magical island of Mont St. Michel, and became lifelong friends.

Back in Paris again, I studied drawing at the Académie Julian in the rue Dragon; but as most of the professors left the city in August for their *congé*, there was little instruction. Dale took a course at the Cordon Bleu and experimented in our little kitchen—using the Leggetts as guinea pigs for her recipes—but often enough when dusk came we'd go out to cafés and restaurants, living *la vie bohème*. An aspiring writer himself, Jack had a job waiting for him in the public relations department at Houghton Mifflin in Boston, so the Leggetts returned to the States. It was autumn and we'd been honeymooning for almost six months. While I felt I should be starting a new book, I had no idea what it would be about.

Meanwhile, over the summer of 1949, Sinclair Lewis had returned to Williamstown, where he began to drink heavily. He became furious with Bennett Cerf and several editors who suggested that his novel-in-progress, *Over the Body of Lucy Jade,* needed drastic revisions. Seeking a back-up opinion, Cerf enlisted Ida Kay to read the manuscript and to deliver a verdict. When she bravely concurred with Bennett's diagnosis, Lewis exploded. Ida Kay remembered the two men fighting at two a.m.: "One hurt, wounded, almost destroyed (Lewis), the other (Cerf) truly trying to save a man's literary reputation...but unable to communicate with a wounded animal."[69]

As the alcohol poisoned his mind, Red developed a new habit: Sleepwalking. A whiskey-swigging wraith had been unleashed on Thorvale Farm. The big fear was that he would fall down the stairs, so they moved his bed to the library downstairs, my old writing studio. Doctors prescribed sleeping pills and intravenous feeding. Wilson Perkins was told to keep an eye on him, day and night.

One night Red began ranting, and a frightened Wilson summoned Ida from her house in the village. She wrote to me years later in 1977: "That night Red was truly drunk…While Wilson went out to the kitchen for a much-needed rest and some food, I tried desperately to keep Red from more drinking."[70]

To distract Red from the liquor cabinet, Ida proposed a game of chess. "Finally in desperation I asked about his Childe Hassam paintings, pointing out the one I liked the best and asking him how and why he had decided on collecting that particular artist. Red immediately screamed…for Wilson, demanding that he remove the painting from the wall immediately and GIVE IT TO ME." (Ida refused to accept the gift.)[71]

Then Red proposed something bigger: He turned to Ida one day and said, "Darling, you have added enormously to my life during these past years." And then, after a pause, "How about going to Europe with me as Mrs. Sinclair Lewis?" Ida, who was half his age, gently declined.[72]

However, Red confided to Bennett Cerf that he'd proposed to Ida and was puzzled by her rejection. Bennett telephoned Ida and said, "God, Ida, I can think of hundreds of beautiful chicks in New York alone who would grab the chance and scream 'aye' without having even seen the man." He added, "You know it won't be for long, the way he's going. And you have so much to give each other."[73]

Ida wouldn't relent, and Red seemed to accept her decision. He began talking about returning to Europe for good. And she recalled him expressing his hatred for Williamstown, saying bitterly, "I've given my life to this country in the best way, and no one cares."[74]

On September 7, 1949, Red Lewis sailed back to Europe aboard the *Nieuw Amsterdam* accompanied by his brother, Dr. Claude Lewis. With his palsied hands Red appeared a sick man, shuffling with the splayed feet characteristic of polyneuritis. He and his brother first toured England, then the Netherlands and Belgium, before catching a train to Paris.

When I learned that Red had arrived in Paris on October 25, I called him at the Hôtel Meurice, and he insisted we have dinner. The following night, Dale and I borrowed our landlord's Citroën, drove across the Seine to the Right Bank, and parked in the Rue de Rivoli. There we met up with Red and Claude in their grand suite on the fifth floor overlooking the Tuileries. Red was very taken with Dale, who, ever the pre-med student, asked him about the laboratory research for *Arrowsmith*.

"Claude here's the real doctor in the family," he said, patting his older brother's shoulder.

A few inches shorter than Red, Claude Lewis was, a stout, jolly small-town Minnesota doctor who smoked cigars. He still had reddish hair and, although six years older than Red, he looked ten years younger.

"Today I'm not a doctor—I'm a tourist on vacation," said Claude, with an easy laugh. "And, boy, my feet are sure sore!" He had spent the day wandering the city and had ridden the elevator to the top of the Eiffel Tower. "There was a strong cold wind blowing out of the northwest, and you could feel the tower sway. No mist or haze today—a great view. But it cost me three hundred francs!"

A few minutes later we were joined by John Mowinckel, a foreign correspondent for the *U.S. News*, and his Italian wife Letitia, whom Red had befriended in Italy that winter. With them was James Campbell, an old friend of Red's. In his early sixties, Campbell was the sort of American who develops an English accent after years of wandering the Continent with no visible means of support.

"All right," said Red. "Let's get this show on the road before we all starve to death."

We went down through the lobby and into the Rue de Rivoli. The Lewis brothers piled into our Citroën while the Mowinckels took James Campbell in their brand-new Studebaker—a novelty in post-War Paris. Red had only been in Paris two days but seemed jubilant—almost frenetically so—to be back in the city he'd first visited during his early triumphs in the 1920s. As we left the hotel he kept peering out the window, commenting on how the streets had changed or remained the same.

Sinclair Lewis first saw Paris in 1922, shortly after *Main Street* had made him famous. His guide was Harold Stearns, an influential American bohemian who took him on a drunken romp through the cafés of Montparnasse. Lewis's fame as a popular writer didn't necessarily endear him to the intellectual expat crowd at Le Dôme, even if Malcolm Cowley was somewhat amused by the inebriated Lewis's impersonation of his own literary character, George Babbitt: "Garçong! Come here you bloody garçong!...Garçong! The lazy frog. Let me tell you, they'd give better service in Zenith. Gentlemen, have you ever been in the Zenith Athletic

Club? Say, that's a swell joint for you..."[75]

Now as we drove toward the Place de la Concorde, Red said, "I need some air." He rolled down the window, craning his head into the breeze like an old bloodhound on vacation.

"First time I've really been in Paris in twenty years," he said. "Going to take you to a marvelous little place on the Left Bank where we all used to go. You'll love it—gay, stimulating—all the good artists, writers go there, the top newspapermen, the thinkers."

We crossed the Seine and, after asking a few pedestrians, arrived at the address in Montparnasse. I let everyone out and parked the car down the street. It was a miserable and dirty little café with only one customer— a student who was reading a book by the light of a candle stuck in a bottle.

"This can't be the place!" Red exclaimed.

Dale checked the address and the name (which I've forgotten, alas), and it was correct.

"But where is Madame Blanc?" Red asked the bored-looking waiter.

"Dead these fifteen years."

"Sixteen," chimed in the student, who might have been Madame Blanc's grandson.

The seven of us squeezed around a table and Red ordered drinks and wine. I had never seen him drink before. It was astonishing to watch him down a whole brandy in a single sucking sound. He had three drinks to our single glass of wine, and kept frowning as he looked around the dingy café.

"This is simply not the place," he repeated irritably, "that's all there is to it. The other place was far bigger—brightly lit, with music, full of people. Not it at all."

Mowinckel was a Norwegian who had been born in Venice, educated in U.S. and spoke four languages. The previous evening he and his wife had taken Red and Claude on a bibulous tour of nightlife in the Latin Quarter. The country doctor commented, "I guess you have to be an *artiste* to get a bang out of that scene."

James Campbell was a pleasant fellow, who, thanks to a small inheritance, did little but stroll the boulevards or sit in cafés watching life go by. Lewis's son Michael would later describe him as "that worn-out old expatriate, shabby friend of shabby contessas and marchesas."[76] But there was something charming about him, and he was sweet to Dale, asking about her "recipe pilgrimage."

The mussels and veal steaks were delicious, as Claude declared several times with gusto, but Red barely touched his food, pushing it around on his plate in his usual fashion, then lighting up a cigarette. The stewed pears for dessert were fine.

Red kept drinking. Steadily. As we ate our meal, the waiter routinely brought an old ledger that served as a guest book, full of names from the past. On one yellowed page I saw the signatures of John Dos Passos, Dorothy Thompson, and Sinclair Lewis. I tried to show the page to Red but he wouldn't look at it.

"Matter of fact," he said as he motioned the waiter for another brandy, "I remember now—wasn't even on this street. Entirely different part of town."

Somehow we got into a discussion with the student. Red invited him over and asked him a great many questions about his life and studies. The student didn't introduce himself and neither did we. He spoke English well but with a heavy accent. He was a literature major and was very serious behind his thick glasses.

"And what American writers do you read?" Red asked, too casually.

The student thought for a moment, then said, "My favorites are Fitzgerald, Hemingway, Steinbeck and Sinclair…"

Red's face lit up. "Ah! Sinclair—"

"Upton Sinclair," continued the youth.

"Uh-huh…" Red frowned and cleared his throat uncomfortably. "Any others?"

The student shrugged. "I've read them all. But those are the ones I most admire."

We left the café and Claude bade us goodnight, hitching a ride back to the hotel with the Mowinckels. But Red wanted more of Paris. "Come on, you honeymooners, the night's still young. Let's go to the Dôme!"

In our car Red mimicked the student's accent and manner to perfection: "My fahvoreets ahr Feetzgerohl, Emeenwhy, Stynabecque, an'"—here he departed slightly from the original—"An' thees Seenclair, thees Seenclair Loowees."

Dale and I flashed each other incredulous looks.

I parked just off the Boulevard Montparnasse and we walked to the Café du Dôme. Campbell, a more a café moth than a barfly, heralded the headwaiter, who seemed to know this cordial ex-pat, and we were led to a prime table.

Campbell enjoyed drinking, to be sure, but he paced himself carefully, savoring the cognac with small sips. In contrast, Red was belting them back. After ordering another round he rehashed the student-in-the-restaurant story for Campbell, embellishing it shamelessly.

"And then that fella says, 'My fahvoreet nohvell off thees Seenclair Loowees ees how-you-call-heem, *Ahrohsmeet.*'"

"One of your best books, Red," said Campbell. "Probably inspired a generation of microbe hunters."

Dale stifled a giggle and pinched me. It was funny in a sad way.

I looked around the café at the interesting characters, some of whom might have been writers or artists; quite a few were American. Red also scanned the room.

"Well, not much has changed in this joint," he said. "Lot of literary poseurs… but at least that sonovabitch Harold Stearns is long gone.…"

Harold Stearns, a notorious freeloader and snob, had in fact died in 1943. But in 1925, when Sinclair Lewis returned to Paris after the success of *Babbitt*, his antics as a big shot author had so infuriated Stearns that he turned the intellectual expat crowd at Le Dôme against him. It didn't help that Lewis would stand up in the café and drunkenly crow that he was equal to Flaubert as a writer and "artist." The next time he and his then-wife Gracie came to Paris, they stayed for over two months at a hotel off the Champs-Elysées, "as far as possible from the Dôme and other haunts of Harold Stearns," as Red wrote to H.L. Mencken.[77]

"Isn't this where you and Robert McAlmon and Hemingway used to come?" I asked.

"We all used to come here," he said, exhaling smoke. "But I was always at a different table. Never met Hemingway in Paris. Not til Cuba, 1940. At his place. Never belonged in their group, never belonged to any group. Never belonged to anybody."

He awkwardly put his gangly arm around Dale. "Now if I'd only had a beautiful little sweet wife like this, the whole story'd be different. I might have been a *great* writer."

Dale was a good sport about Red's harmless flirting, but it pained me to watch my mentor, this once-great author, turn into a drunken self-caricature. At a certain point I made eye contact with James Campbell and suggested it might be time to go.

"All right, Red," said Campbell. "Let's call it a night, shall we?"

We walked to the car, and I got Red settled in the back seat. I offered a lift to Campbell, but he said he'd prefer walking to wherever he was heading, no doubt another café. It was just a little after ten and, after all, this was Paris.

We drove to the Hôtel Meurice and I enlisted the doorman to guide *monsieur* Lewis up the steps. At the entrance Red turned, waved his skeletal hand, and stumbled into the lobby.

The following day, Red sobered up enough to write to Ida Kay back in Williamstown:

> Did see Barney. His wife is pretty & charming, small beside B's bulk, but (of course) with twice his will & industry. But fond of him. I don't think their writing–sketching–Europe venture has been too successful, & now they are heading back to California.[78]

Three days later Red and Claude invited us to eat at a restaurant a few blocks from the Meurice. It was a little Chinese place, a busy Friday night and I could tell he'd already had a few drinks. He only mentioned the unfinished Booth book once. ("Just write the damn thing and fulfill our contract!") We ate a plain noodle soup, some chicken chow mein, and consumed several bottles of wine, though Dale drank little and Claude drank none. While we ate dessert, *tarte tatin* with cream, Red drained a whole bottle of wine himself.

As we parted on the street, the usually cheerful Claude turned to me and whispered, "I'm worried about Hal. If he keeps drinking like this he'll be dead in a year."

CHAPTER ELEVEN

RED'S LAST DAYS

Dale and I returned to San Francisco and heard no more from or about Sinclair Lewis, except for bits of news in letters from Ida Kay. It wasn't until after his death, mainly from the Schorer and Lingeman biographies and Red's letters (scattered among various American libraries), that I learned how he spent his final years.

In November of 1949, Lewis began moving from town to town in Italy with a car and driver. He was having a drink and a smoke in a hotel lobby in Assisi, when he struck up a conversation with a charming dark-haired stranger in his late-thirties, Alexander ("Alec") Manson, who said he worked for the Thomas Cook travel agency and had served ten years in British military intelligence. He referred to himself as Major Manson (though later information indicates he was but a sergeant major). A few more drinks and Lewis hired Manson as his final personal secretary/companion.[79]

Lewis took Manson to Florence, where he rented La Villa Costa about ten minutes outside of the city. Built in 1939 by a Fascist tycoon, it was an overwrought, tacky mansion, but its tower offered a breathtaking view of olive groves and the spires of Florence. Inside, there was a grand balustrade of milky Venetian glass pillars, gilded fixtures, and black and white marble floors in a checkerboard pattern.

Brother Claude and Red's second son Michael—now six-foot five-inches tall and an adventurous lad of nineteen—came for Christmas in Florence. James Campbell, Red's shabby-genteel friend whom we'd met in Paris, also turned up. From time to time, Lewis would rave to Campbell about the wonderful time they would have when his health improved. But when depressed, he would moan, "No one has ever been so unhappy."[80]

Impressed by Manson's charm and polished European ways, Red

wrote to Ida on February 1, 1950:

> Alexander Manson is the only good secretary I have ever had, and I hope to God he'll stay with me the rest of my life. In efficiency, he makes all the Barney Conrads look like fools; in intelligence and amusingness, makes them look like dolts.
>
> He is half English—his father was a London solicitor, and he went to London University and had started in Oxford when war broke out—but he is half Polish, which beautifully alters that stiff British superciliousness I have always disliked…Alex recently finished ten years in the intelligence section of the British army, the last 5 years in Trieste, in Italy…He speaks French and German (these he learned as a boy in school in Switzerland) and Italian as well as he does English. In all business and domestic affairs, he is astonishingly quick and efficient and dependable, but socially he is charming, and with something to say….You'll be certain to fall in love with him."[81]

By March, 1950, Red Lewis was working nine hours and smoking four packs of cigarettes a day. Perhaps regretting his harsh words to Bennett Cerf about the weak *Lucy Jade* novel, he began dramatically rewriting it with a new title: *World So Wide*. He eliminated the Lucy Jade character, bolstered the central character—a successful architect—and re-introduced the title character from *Dodsworth*.

Though he wrote upbeat reports to his friends at home, the alcohol and cigarettes had taken a toll; he suffered a minor heart attack and an Italian doctor was treating him with injections of liver extract, glucose, and vitamins—typical remedies for the effects of alcoholism. One visiting physician, Dr. Vincenzo Lapiccirella, noticed that a bedside water carafe was filled with whiskey. Later, as Lewis began consulting him for therapeutic talk sessions, the doctor commented, "Only geniuses and kings are as lonely as Red Lewis."[82]

Manson claimed to have moderated Lewis's drinking, switching him from whiskey to wine, but by most reliable accounts of this time Lewis swallowed a bottle at lunch and another at dinner. Admirably, Red managed to transform *World So Wide* into a revealing tale of an older

American betrayed by love and his own restless dreams, but it did not measure up to his hard-hitting masterpieces of the Twenties and Thirties.

Manson and his girlfriend, Tina Lazzerini, laid out plans for a rather self-serving grand tour that would take Lewis to Paris, then Naples, Sicily and even Egypt, and convinced the author to buy a brand-new Studebaker Champion as a touring car. The former tightwad was now throwing money around haphazardly, buying an expensive wardrobe from Dior for Lazzerini and allowing Manson to handle all financial matters.

In July, 1950, Carl Van Doren died of a heart attack. Lewis himself suffered two minor heart attacks in Zurich that summer. When Ida Kay arrived in late July for her own long-awaited European tour, she put aside her travel plans and ended up caring for Red. Though trapped in his Zurich hotel as an invalid, he thoughtfully arranged for Ida to play on a local golf course. She was astonished at the jewelry and couture clothing Red had given Tina Lazzerini, but was more shocked by the author's physical deterioration. Red asked her to sell Thorvale for as little fifty thousand dollars, just to be rid of it. Furthermore, he said, he would never go back to Williamstown or the United States. "Europe is home to me now."[83]

After visiting Naples, in the fall of 1950, Lewis grew so exhausted that Manson parked him in Rome. There he resumed writing a few hours a day, working on *The Enchantment of Elaine Kent,* a novel about an American girl who marries an Italian. As Lewis's health declined, Manson kept such tight control over him that when his wayward son Michael Lewis arrived from London a few minutes late for dinner, Manson abruptly turned him away at the door.

On the last day of 1950, Red Lewis awakened early. As Manson reported later, "He worked from six to eight a.m., then had his usual big breakfast of porridge, honey, bread and butter, and sat in the living room. Suddenly he staggered to the door of my room and said, 'Alec, something terrible is happening. I am going to die.' I lead him to a big chair, and there he buried his head in my arms like a frightened child. Those were his last fully conscious words."[84]

Red was taken to the Clinica Electrica where he grew delirious, and suffered such violent convulsions that it took six people to hold him down. Though doctors stabilized him, on January 10, 1951 he suffered a massive heart attack and died. He was sixty-five.

A few weeks after Red Lewis died, I learned of a final macabre vignette: A friend of mine went into the U.S. Embassy at Rome and saw a consular official down on her knees with a broom and pan. "What are you doing?" he asked.

"Sweeping up Sinclair Lewis," was the answer.

Red's ashes had been entrusted to an Embassy safe pending final disposal. While being transferred for shipment home, the silver urn had tipped over, spilling bone and ash across the marble floor.

The funeral service was held in Sauk Centre, Minnesota, attended by Claude and the rest of the Lewis clan, a small band of well-wishers, and a few reporters. I was not there. (Nor did Alec Manson attend). Ida Kay, bless her heart, took the train from Williamstown to be there. She wrote simply in her short memoir:

> In the bitter cold, snow-covered Greenwood Cemetery, out among the fields but less than a mile from Main Street, Claude clipped the green ribbon on the silver urn that held his brother's ashes. His gloved hand fumbled with the cover; he lifted the top and bent quickly to pour the ashes into the grave. Even here, there was nothing funereal. If anyone was sad, there were no tears to show it. Stepping back from the edge of the grave, Claude said, "Let's say the Lord's Prayer, quickly." With hands pressed to half-frozen ears some said it more quickly than others, and the Lord's Prayer echoed like an English round into eternity.
>
> "The whole thing was good; I say, the whole thing was good," Claude observed in his usual clipped, cheery tone as soon as we had settled in his car. "That hot coffee down there at the high school will taste mighty good."[85]

CHAPTER TWELVE

LIFE AFTER LEWIS

Back in San Francisco Dale and I were living on Arguello Street, a wide boulevard near the entrance to the Presidio. I was getting portrait commissions, teaching writing in night school, and writing short stories and articles, mainly on bullfighting. We kept house with a pet flying squirrel and a huge tank of seahorses which we were breeding for money. Referring to a black & white photo and the portrait sketch of Red I'd started at Thorvale, I painted a full-blown portrait of him in oil. It now hung in our back hallway—a constant reminder of his writerly discipline and my own shortcomings.

When I learned of Red's death in January 1951, I immediately regretted not corresponding more often with him. A month later I wrote to Ida Kay, "I have been thinking of doing a novel based on that summer, twisting things around a bit but using Red as a model. I'm just kicking it around in my head now, but I was thinking of getting Marcella into it, that is her leaving him for a young man—maybe his secretary, instead of Mike [Amrine]—and his going off to Europe, again the lonely searcher."[86]

But another book was already bubbling inside my brain. About a year after Sinclair Lewis died I put a sheet of paper in the typewriter and my fingers began to type:

A novel starting in the morning and ending at the end of the bullfight—just seven hours—no flashbacks, just every single thing that happens in that day, everything that happens in the fight, the character to be like Manolete, a loner, ugly, over the hill but unable to step down from being *El Número Uno*. Not a bad title…

Ever since I'd learned of Manolete's death, a book had been germinating in my mind. Now it demanded to be written. I quickly outlined chapters for *A Day of Fear*. Once I'd started typing, I couldn't stop. It was hard to sleep at night as the ideas tumbled from my brain. Many times I awakened poor Dale, very pregnant with our first child, by turning on the light to scribble some phrase or detail. At the first sign of dawn I would dart into my studio and stay there all day.

The writing process was different than it had ever been. I seemed to have caught fire, driven by a feverish compulsion. When I sat at the typewriter I didn't ask myself, "How would Hemingway—or Sinclair Lewis—write this?" I just chose the most direct, graphic way. Day after day this exhilarating process consumed me. *Writers like us*.

In eight weeks the book was finished. I was exhausted, not so much from the labor as from re-living that terrible day so totally alone with my protagonist. I wasn't sure how good a book it was, but I knew it was the best thing I'd written. Dale thought so, too. Full of confidence, I sent it off to Marcella, who presented it to Random House.

The following week a wire came from the editor, Robert Linscott. I tore open the envelope and read:

VERY SORRY, NOT QUITE ENTHUSIASTIC ENOUGH ABOUT A DAY OF FEAR TO PUBLISH. RETURNING MANUSCRIPT.

This was the end.

The house that had published *The Innocent Villa* had rejected me. It made me suspect that Bennett Cerf had published my first book only as a favor to his best-selling author, Sinclair Lewis.

Maybe *A Day of Fear* was simply not good enough for hardcover. I'd heard of a second-rate paperback firm that was looking for novels and might pay five hundred or even eight hundred dollars for my shabby effort. Of course that would be it—no further royalties. I was about to submit it when Dale, believing the book deserved better, said, "Why not get Jack's opinion?" Jack Leggett, whom we'd met on our honeymoon in Paris, was in the public relations department at Houghton Mifflin. I mailed the manuscript to him, but with no real hope.

A week later a wire came from Paul Brook, the head of Houghton Mifflin:

ABSOLUTELY DELIGHTED WITH YOUR NOVEL DAY OF
FEAR. HOPE YOU WILL ALSO ILLUSTRATE IT.
HOWEVER WITH YOUR PERMISSION WE WOULD LIKE
TO CHANGE THE TITLE TO MATADOR. PLAN TO
PUBLISH SOONEST. ONE THOUSAND DOLLARS
ADVANCE ON ITS WAY TO YOU.

We were jubilant. Throughout the following months a string of
miraculous wires arrived. *Reader's Digest* Condensed Books bought the
novel for a $20,000 advance. The Book of the Month Club took *Matador*
for $25,000. *The New York Times Book Review* featured it on the front
page. *The Saturday Review* raved, *Time* Magazine gave it two gushing
pages, and the *Chicago Tribune*'s Victor Hass hailed it as "More than a
novel about a man—it *is* the man.... like something by Goya."[87]

Dell Publishing bought the paperback rights for $22,000, the highest
price it had ever paid. *Matador* became the number one best seller in
America, and the foreign rights took my little story into France, Italy,
Germany, Holland, Scandinavia and Argentina—a dozen countries in as
many weeks.

And finally there was a telegram from José Ferrer:

JOHN HUSTON AND MY POSITION VERY SIMPLE. WE
WISH TO BUY AND MAKE MATADOR INTO A FINE
MOTION PICTURE WITH YOU DOING THE SCREENPLAY.
WILL PAY ANY REASONABLE PRICE. CAN YOU COME
TO HOLLYWOOD TO DISCUSS?

Success had come to little Barny Conrad, aged thirty, and all was rosy.
Or was it?

There was only one person missing—Sinclair Lewis. I wished he were
still alive, not only to share his pupil's glory, but to offer advice on
handling overnight success. *Writers—like us.*

I handled it badly. Other writers of my generation had been sacrificed
on the altar of the bitch-goddess Success. Tom Heggen's war novel *Mister
Roberts* (1946) was a bestseller, a hit play on Broadway and a big movie
starring Henry Fonda, when he killed himself in the bathtub with booze
and barbiturates. Ross Lockridge, Jr., author of the 1066-page novel

Raintree County (bestseller, play and film) chose a similar exit in 1948 by carbon monoxide poisoning. (In 1974, my friend Jack Leggett wrote a dual biography of these writers.)

While *Matador* was flying off the bookshelves, my marriage with Dale was flying off the rails. I went down to Hollywood to negotiate with John Huston and José Ferrer, rented a bungalow and took up with an old girlfriend who had surfaced in Los Angeles. High on success, I wanted to fly higher and began swallowing enormous amounts of booze, uppers and downers. Realizing what a big mistake I'd made, I retreated to San Francisco, frightened that I was completely out of control. I felt like was being sucked down a giant soul-killing drain and my sanity was on the line. I urgently needed help. I drove to the hospital where I ran into Dale's pediatrician, of all people.

"Dr. Marsh," I said. "I am very, very sick. I am losing my mind. I need to sleep, desperately."

That's the last I remember. Later, I was told, I went berserk. They stuck me with a massive hypo and wrapped me in a straitjacket. They took me to a sanitarium outside the city where I spent a week manacled to a bed. A distinguished neurologist recommended shock treatment. "It's a clear-cut case of alcohol and barbiturate poisoning," he said, "and shock will get him out of it." Dale's authorization was required, and she gave it. I was wheeled into the treatment room a maniac, the cathodes were attached to my head, and they flicked the switch. Thirty minutes later I emerged a rational human asking, "Where am I? How'd I get here?"

After a two-week recovery, I was discharged and went home. A month later I was back in Hollywood again, this time with no alcohol, pills, or girlfriend. Ferrer and Huston paid me $50,000 for the motion picture rights to *Matador* (though the picture has yet to be made).

As for the novel, the kudos kept coming. When *The Saturday Review* asked a dozen famous authors to name the year's best book, John Steinbeck chose *Matador*. We'd never met, but I wrote him an admiring letter of thanks. He sent a warm letter back that said in part: "I like bullfights, because to me it is a lonely, formal anguished microcosm of what happens to every man, sometimes even in an office strangled by the glue on the envelopes. In the bull ring he survives for awhile—

sometimes." Steinbeck's words might easily have applied to a writer's life.

It took many months to repair my marriage. My first child Barnaby had been born April 18, 1952, and I felt a new kind of joy watching him crawl around the rug of our new house on Bay Street. I tried to keep a serious writing schedule while also developing a reputation as a portrait painter. But when I started a nightclub, El Matador, in San Francisco's North Beach in 1953, my evenings became devoted to a drinking crowd that fed my ego and tempted me in other ways. Dale and I eventually had two more children, Cayetana and Winston, despite my wild straying and hangovers. Sometimes, when booze got the best of me, I looked at my portrait of a haggard Sinclair Lewis and abstained for weeks. But I was young and strong, right? I could handle it.

Matador was eventually translated into over twenty-five languages. After that success, my publishers encouraged me to chronicle the world of bullfighting I knew so well. I traveled frequently to Spain and Mexico and wrote six books on the subject, including *La Fiesta Brava, Gates of Fear,* and the *Encyclopedia of Bullfighting.* Yet these were non-fiction, and the real challenge for a writer, I felt, was the novel, a work of art more true and lasting than even the best-written reportage or history.

It wasn't until 1960—nine years after I'd first told Ida Kay about my idea to write about Red Lewis—that I began my novel about a great American author in the twilight of his life. I recast Red as Winston "Mug" Dangerfield, winner of two Pulitzer Prizes, who is ensconced at his great estate, "Senlac," in the hills above Santa Barbara. Dangerfield is on the wagon, hoping to bolster his flagging career with one last masterpiece—and to keep his young mistress Lucha from leaving him. Then his estranged twenty-two-year-old son, David Copperfield Dangerfield, appears. Resentful of the father who has ignored him most of his life and intrigued by the sultry Lucha, David cuckolds his father and is soon embroiled in a triangle that would have interested Freud. I found the book easy to write—I could hear Lewis's cantankerous Midwestern voice ranting throughout it—but I needed to alter the character, to make him my own creation.

When Truman Capote visited San Francisco in 1961, we met for lunch at Enrico's with my old friend Herb Caen, the witty three-dot columnist who invented the word "beatnik." After the triumph of *Breakfast at Tiffany's*, Truman was researching a non-fiction crime story that would soon become *In Cold Blood*. Over several drinks, he asked what I was working on.

"A novel called *Dangerfield*," I said.

"Gorgeous title!" he said. "And why is the field dangerous?"

"It's one word," I said. "It's the man's name."

"Oh, no, no, no, no!" he said. "It must be two words! *Danger Field*!"

"But it's the main character's name," I protested.

"Change it," Truman said. "Rename him Smedrood and call the book *Danger Field*!"

For better or worse, I didn't take his advice.

By July 1961, I'd nearly finished the manuscript when Ernest Hemingway killed himself with a shotgun at his home in Ketchum, Idaho. His suicide side-swiped me. I had idolized him, and his masterful book on bullfighting had changed my life. Both Lewis and Hemingway had influenced my approach to writing and, it would seem, my life as a two-fisted drinker. Now both were dead. As I turned forty, I wondered not just about the writing life, but my personal conduct. *Writers like us.*

There were problems at home, too. Dale, who rightly mistrusted my nightclub, had grown passionate about horses and wanted to move to the country, while I still needed the city and all the stimulation—good and bad—that San Francisco offered. I began having an affair. In 1962, Dale and I divorced. Within a year I was married again, to Mary Nobles Slater, whom I'd met on a tennis court in Marin. She was twenty-eight, divorced with two children, and loved to travel.

Dangerfield appeared to generally good reviews, with *The New York Times* reviewer David Dempsey giving it some applause, and *Harper's* calling it "a brilliant job." It was obvious to many that I'd based the book on Sinclair Lewis, and it did well enough. The theatrical production was another story.

One day the telephone rang in my Telegraph Hill studio. "Hello," said a deep voice. "This is Herman Shumlin calling from New York." I didn't recognize his name at first. Then I realized I was speaking to the director of such stage classics as *Grand Hotel*, *Little Foxes* and *Inherit The Wind*.

"Your novel is written in three acts exactly like a play and I want to do it," Shumlin said. "You have an absolutely fascinating main character here. Let's make it a Broadway play. I want the rights, but I want you to write it!"

The next day, Roger Stevens, producer of *Tea and Sympathy* and *A Man For All Seasons* called to announce that *he* wanted to do it.

The following day Joseph Fields, producer of *Flower Drum Song*, called to say that *he* wanted to do it.

Then the secretary of the legendary Moss Hart called to ask if the rights were available. Finally David Merrick, the titan of Broadway, called and insisted on doing it.

Bedazzled, all I could say was, "I'll talk to my agent and get back to you."

The outcome was that Roger L. Stevens joined forces with Herman Shumlin: Stevens to produce the play, Shumlin to direct it. I then spent four months writing it, being careful, as Shumlin urged continuously, to "preserve all the values and relationships of the novel." Stevens and Shumlin seemed pleased with my efforts and, in preparation for the Broadway launch, lined up Henry Fonda to play Dangerfield and young Peter Fonda as his son David. Then Herman hired Robert Thom, a successful screenwriter, to "add a few additional scenes."

Suddenly, everything about this play changed. First, the Fondas pulled out due to a movie commitment. Soon Thom's version of my script bore almost no resemblance to my novel: Gone was the romance between the old writer's mistress and his son, and most of the characters' names had been inexplicably changed. At least, I consoled myself, the title was still mine. Not for long. Shumlin called me and said, "The lawyers are worried about this man Dangerfield."

Just after my novel was published a rather distinguished-looking man had come into the Matador one evening and introduced himself as George Dangerfield.

"How interesting," I'd said, mentioning the title of my then just-released novel.

"I know," he said.

"But it's about a writer."

"I know," he said. *"I* am a writer."

"But the writer in this book lives in Santa Barbara."

"I know," he said. *"I* live in Santa Barbara."

"But this is about a Pulitzer Prize-winning author," I said.

"I won the Pulitzer Prize for history in 1953," he said. "And your book has caused me a great deal of embarrassment."

Uh-oh. I had never heard of George Dangerfield before.

Now, after Shumlin's anxious call, I telephoned Mr. Dangerfield and asked how he'd feel about a play called *Dangerfield*. His response was, understandably, *antarctic*—especially after "the embarrassment caused by the book." After hanging up, I immediately told Shumlin to change the main character's name to "Smith" and retitle the play *Danger Field* the way Truman Capote had originally suggested for my book.

Instead, in this era of odd titles like *Who's Afraid of Virginia Woolf?*, Shumlin and Thom decided to call it *A Bicycle Ride to Nevada*.

I went East for a week of rehearsals and the opening in New Haven. The results of Thom's surgery were shocking. The Dangerfield character was now "Winston Sawyer," and he pedaled a stationary bike on stage; "Nevada," Thom said, was a metaphor for a "dry" (booze-less) place. Franchot Tone was now playing the lead with Lois Smith as the "Lucha"/Marcella Powers character, and Richard Jordan as his estranged son, David Sawyer. I had worried that Tone, a famous movie star, was too good-looking and suave to play someone based on Sinclair Lewis—and he was—but now the play had even bigger problems thanks to Thom's revisions.

In my book (and my version of the play) Winston Dangerfield was presented early on as a reformed alcoholic who—if he drinks again— would die "as surely as if by a pistol shot." And—in the last chapter of my book—he does drink again, foreshadowing an imminent death.

Robert Thom had compressed the last twenty-four hours of the protagonist's life into three acts. But all the suspense dies in *his* first act when Franchot Tone walks over to the home bar, swallows a whopping tumbler of whiskey—and remains "drunk" throughout the play.

During one of the rehearsals in New Haven, I turned to Shumlin and whispered, "There goes our suspense! Why can't he go over to the bar, pour himself a drink, look at it for a telling moment, then dump it in the sink?"

Shumlin sighed. "This play has become a much different, much bigger thing than your book," he said loftily.

"But you're killing our ending," I said. Thom had injected the play with so many quirks that removed empathy for the characters, disregarded motivations, and avoided conflict that even Roger Stevens sided with me. During the tryouts in New Haven and Philadelphia, Stevens tried in vain to get the play back on track. At times it made me cringe to see what a Frankenstein-esque script we all had concocted around the character inspired by my former mentor, Red Lewis.

The play opened at the Cort Theater on Broadway on September, 24, 1963 to great fanfare. Yes, it was exciting to see stars like Burgess Meredith and Otto Preminger seated among the formally attired audience and, yes, Howard Bay's stage set—an explosion of books—was stunning. I also knew the cast had worked as hard as they could on this show and would give it their best. But by now I was entirely sick of the play.

The minute the audience was seated, I snuck out of the Cort Theater and went around the corner to watch Uta Hagen in Edward Albee's *Who's Afraid of Virginia Woolf?*—a breathtaking performance. At midnight, when I joined the *Bicycle* cast at Sardi's for the traditional party, I could honestly declare, "I've just spent a *wonderful* evening at the theater!"

The reviews were not horrible—not snide, not disastrous—but still bad, except for one by John Chapman, the *Daily News* critic, who loved it. The great Walter Kerr of the *Herald Tribune* opened with this: "I don't think there's a play in 'Bicycle Ride to Nevada,' but there's a sequence toward the end of the second act that comes exasperatingly close to, and then misses, what might have been an extraordinary theatrical effect."

"The play at the Cort, like the Barnaby Conrad novel on which it was based, is plainly indebted to the legend of Sinclair Lewis's later and sorrier years though the central character answers to the name Brick Sawyer. Now Lewis was, among other things, a natural mime. He was also, as I understand it, a perpetual mimic, an unstoppable mimic, a mimic at the drop of a cocktail glass..."

Kerr went on to point out how this exaggerated character flaw weakened the play: "But this odd talent, or trick of the psyche, does not become important until, deep into the play's center, Mr. Tone is at last confronted by his only son, the son he has virtually never seen and certainly never loved. The son is bitter, and possibly—just possibly—loving."

The critic rather gently suggested that if the two characters could speak to each other "something good might come out of it." Instead, this gift of mimicry—"waspish, brutal, totally honest, sloppily evasive"—runs amok, infecting all the players. "Mr. Tone can suddenly without a pause for breath, begin to mimic the son he has just met. Startlingly, Mr. Jordan can mimic Mr. Tone, just as quickly."

Kerr wound it up gracefully: "Author Thom's literary methods have contributed to the stalemate...I still wish that big scene had battered its way through."[88]

Howard Taubman of the *New York Times* pointed out another of the play's weaknesses:

"The problem of writing about a writer—or a composer or painter—is to draw drama from the business of creation. The creative act may be a fierce struggle, but it is unrelievedly private." The review ends with this: "As the old man collapses in time for the final curtain, the son suddenly sheds his demonic frenzy and exclaims piteously that at last he has recaptured his father. Too late for everyone—including the play."[89]

This limping, sleep-walking show mercifully died after one performance. My year-and-a-half-long efforts to bring Sinclair Lewis to life on stage had ended in shambles. Fortunately, I didn't consider myself a playwright. So, it was a relief to return to writing books, an art form where usually one author gets all the credit—or all the blame.

Writers...like us.

CHAPTER THIRTEEN

RED'S LEGACY

Today, it's hard for me to believe that over sixty years have passed since Red Lewis died, and that I may be the last person alive who knew him well. Little by little the *dramatis personae* of Red's circle disappeared.

Ida Kay married a good-hearted Williams College chemistry professor named Charles Compton in 1953. She had an extensive career in publishing, working for the University of Chicago Press and Time, Inc. We corresponded for over thirty-five years and she eventually published (posthumously) a fifty-one-page pamphlet, *Sinclair Lewis at Thorvale Farm*. She died in 1985 at age 68. I will always remember her tan and youthful, backstroking across Red Lewis's swimming pool that summer at Thorvale.

The historian Carl Van Doren died in 1950. Though drama critic and editor George Jean Nathan had published a paean *The Bachelor Life* in 1941, he finally married the younger Julie Haydon in 1955, only to die three years later at age seventy-six.

Alma and Wilson Perkins remained as caretakers of Thorvale for the two years that Red traveled around Europe. When the estate was sold to the Carmelite Fathers as a retreat, Alma stayed on as the Order's cook, and Wilson took a job at a local electric company. They and their daughter Judy continued to live in the little white cottage for a few years, until they moved to Southern California. Cut out of Red's will, Joseph Hardrick died relatively young, sometime in the late 1950s.

Marcella Powers and her husband Michael Amrine gained by Sinclair Lewis's death, according to Red's lifelong friend, Harrison Smith, an editor at *Saturday Review*, who wrote me in August, 1951:

Red's will was interesting. He left half to his son [Michael], in charge of Dorothy until he is 21. One quarter he left to Mrs. Powers for life to be divided on his (sic) [her] death between Marcella, Carl Van Doren, Edith Haggard (his agent) and Joseph, his chauffeur, providing he was in his employ at the time of his death. Since Carl and Joseph are out of the picture, Mrs. Haggard and Marcella inherit one eighth and on Mrs. Powers' death will each hold one quarter of the estate. It is interesting to speculate whether he made a bargain with Mrs. P. when she was his housekeeper and his companion abroad.[90]

As a literary agent, Marcella had a number of successes, including selling the movie rights to *All About Eve* in 1950, but after my novel *Matador* was published, we parted ways. She and Michael Amrine had a son, Mio, who died in an accident in Paris in 1978 at age twenty-one. She eventually divorced and married publicist Edwin Pigeon, had two children with him, and moved to Santa Fe, New Mexico in 1960. She loved Santa Fe, wrote for local magazines, and even appeared on stage in the play *Wings* in 1982, before dying of cancer in 1985. Marcella left some 264 letters from Red Lewis to the library at St. Cloud University in Minnesota. Shortly before her death, Marcella wrote an eloquent tribute to Red and mailed it to his niece, Isabel Lewis Agrell:

> Red was the most courageous man I've ever known. He changed my life in so many ways…he formed my opinions on so many basic issues that I still believe in. I reread some of his books still. And he was good to my mother, whose life was pretty dreary before she met him. She ran a boarding house soon after my father died and worked so hard for so many years and he saw that her later years were comfortable and even glamorous. It was the kind of generous gesture he was always making. He helped so many people in need.[91]

Horace Cayton, Jr. surfaced in San Francisco at the Matador around 1960. He had moved to California to repair ties with his estranged brother, Revels, a firebrand labor leader who later became a deputy mayor of San Francisco. Horace was then teaching at UC Berkeley, while writing an autobiography to exorcise the demons of racism, loneliness, and alcoholism that had nearly ruined his life. He was down on his luck financially so I put him in touch with a local philanthropist, Mortimer Fleischacker, who advanced him enough money to finish *Long Old Road*, an extraordinary, heartbreaking memoir (with a chapter devoted to Lewis). This success led to a commissioned biography of his good friend, the late novelist Richard Wright. While conducting research in Paris in 1970, Horace died of natural causes at age sixty-seven. I still cherish the gentleness and humor he shared during those days at Thorvale Farm.

Though I never met him, Walter White, the inspiration for *Kingsblood Royal*, built the NAACP into a respected organization. His great legacy was to have drafted President Truman's presidential order to desegregate the armed forces after World War Two. Shortly after publishing his autobiography, *A Man Called White,* in 1948, Walter White divorced his black wife, Gladys, to marry a white magazine editor from South Africa. He died of a heart attack at age sixty-one, in 1955.

I didn't get to New York much, but from time to time—while staying at the Algonquin Hotel—I'd read that Jane White was appearing in various acting venues. In 1959, she originated the role of Queen Aggravain (opposite a young Carol Burnett as the princess) in the Broadway musical *Once Upon a Mattress.* She had several major roles in the 1965 Shakespeare festival and won an Obie, but there was a paucity of roles for black actors. She starred in *The Edge of Night* and several other television soap operas and played the teacher (Lady Jones) in the 1998 film version of Toni Morrison's *Beloved.* Jane was happily married to an Italian writer and restaurateur, and continued to play theaters around the country, but without achieving the stardom she dreamed of. She died at 88 in the summer of 2011.

Bennett Cerf continued to make Random House one of the great publishers of the twentieth century. Twenty-two years after buying my first book, Bennett published my 1969 autobiography, *Fun While It Lasted* (in which he also appears). He died at seventy-three of a heart attack in 1971, but left his own insightful, rollicking memoir of the publishing world, *At Random.* Once asked what his epitaph might be Bennett replied: "He left people a little happier than they were when he came into the room." He lived that credo throughout his life.

Red's former wife, Dorothy Thompson (whom I never met), was married happily to Czechoslovakian artist Maxim Kopf until she died of a heart attack in 1961 while visiting Portugal.

Red's first wife, Grace Hegger Lewis, never really got over the death of their son Wells, but she had a happy marriage to Telesforo Casanova, living in Manhattan. In 1955 Gracie wrote a memoir of her years with Red, *With Love from Gracie*, which ended with this tender farewell: "Dear, dear Minnesota Tumbleweed, driven by the winds of your own blowing, rootless to the day when your ashes were returned to the soil which had never received your living roots, I offer you these memories." We corresponded off and on until her death in 1981. (Telesforo died later that year of burns and smoke inhalation from a fire in their apartment.)

Michael Lewis, Red's son by Dorothy Thompson, studied acting at the Royal Academy of Dramatic Art in London, battled alcoholism, married twice, and fathered two sons, John Paul and Gregory Claude, and a daughter Lesley. Michael died in 1985 of Hodgkin's lymphoma. Gregory Claude went into the construction business and John Paul became a writer of historical novels.[92]

Red's brother, Dr. Claude Lewis, continued to travel around the world and practiced medicine into his seventies, before dying in 1957.

Alexander ("Alec") Manson, Red's last secretary, wrote an essay, "The Last Days of Sinclair Lewis," for *The Saturday Evening Post*, published on March 31, 1951; but later he refused to be interviewed by the distinguished Lewis biographer, Mark Schorer. Manson and his girlfriend, Tina Lazzerini, simply disappeared into Europe. James Campbell, the charming ex-pat in Paris, did speak to biographer Mark Schorer, but I never heard what became of Campbell.

In the late 1950s, Schorer (who never met Red) interviewed me for his monumental biography of Sinclair Lewis. When the book came out in 1961, I was somewhat dismayed to read his assessment of Red:

> He was one of the worst writers in modern American literature, but without his writing one cannot imagine modern American literature. That is because, without his writing, we can hardly imagine ourselves.[93]

Schorer may have been too harsh on Lewis, but with time his assessment has proven true from an aesthetic point of view. Red was a bold provocateur and skilled chronicler of our country, but he was not a poet, stylist, or artist, and time passed him by. As the Sixties unfolded, Norman Mailer, Gore Vidal, Saul Bellow, William Styron, Joan Didion, and Joseph Heller replaced such giants of American literature as Hemingway and Faulkner, pushing Lewis's fame deeper into obscurity.

Yet Lewis—as an iconic literary figure—remained on the scene.

Sherman Yellen wrote a play about Lewis and Dorothy Thompson called *Strangers* which opened in January 1979 in New York. I watched a rehearsal with my eldest son Barnaby. The lead actor, Bruce Dern, known for portraying psychopaths, caught the author's mannerisms so perfectly—lurching around the stage in Red's manic loose-jointed way, smoking like a chimney, braying with that high-pitched twang—that I could have sworn my old employer had risen from the dead.

The play begins with Red and Dorothy (played by Lois Nettleton) during their love-struck moments in Berlin—when he proposed marriage on their first date—then moves to Moscow where he insults the Communists, then on to their Vermont farm where he drinks too much and can't write, then back to Europe where she exposes the Third Reich and he again drinks too much; then he wins the Nobel Prize and drinks again. Near the end of the play Red is forced into a straitjacket and launches into a long monologue about being a disappointment to his doctor-father. The characters argue and bicker up a storm, but bickering isn't dramatic conflict, and the play limped along for nine performances before closing. While it was a reminder of my own disastrous theatrical experience with *Dangerfield*, I was thrilled by the intensity of Bruce Dern's performance. His portrayal of Sinclair Lewis was spot-on.

As for Lewis's novels: In 1992 The Library of America published *Main Street* and *Babbitt* in a single 898-page volume, edited by John Hersey, which prompted Gore Vidal to skewer Lewis —as only Vidal could—in a *New York Review of Books* essay:

Sinclair Lewis seems to have dropped out of what remains of world literature. The books are little read today, and he's seldom discussed in his native land outside his hometown, Sauk Centre,

Minnesota…Lewis's books are on the shelves of the town library. For the most part, that's where they stay.[94]

And yet, as Vidal noted, Lewis's titles and characters—like those of Dickens—have become part of our language: *Main Street*, *Babbitt*, *Arrowsmith*, *Elmer Gantry*, and *It Can't Happen Here*.

In 1955, his first wife Grace Hegger Casanova astutely observed that though Lewis's books have a recognizable style built of intense observation, "It is significant that he created no school of writing as have Hemingway and Faulkner, Henry James and Flaubert. He influenced public thinking rather than public writing."[95]

Though Lewis's novels remain in print, at the beginning of the twenty-first century they are largely relegated to college reading lists. Was anyone reading *Babbitt* or *Main Street* anymore?

"Oh, yes," said Sally E. Parry, editor of *The Sinclair Lewis Society Newsletter*, published by Illinois State University. "Along with *Elmer Gantry* and *Dodsworth*."

Sally invited me to be the keynote speaker of the Sinclair Lewis Society's annual meeting in July 2000 at Sauk Centre, Minneapolis. I was warmly welcomed by her group and my talk focused mainly on that summer I'd spent with Red fifty-three years in the past. Later I was shown every site in Sauk Centre that related to Red's life, from his tree-shaded family home to his final resting place in the cemetery, where he is buried between his father and mother, and near his beloved stepmother. (His brother Claude was buried in another cemetery.) I was particularly struck by the simplicity of the inscription on Red's tombstone:

SINCLAIR LEWIS

1885-1951

AUTHOR OF "MAIN STREET"

While he'd pilloried his provincial birthplace in that great novel, he brought fame to a dirt-road prairie town that once predicted that Doc Lewis's skinny red-headed kid wouldn't amount to much—even if he did go off to a fancy place like Yale. That day, there were plenty of flowers at his grave and the town enthusiastically promotes itself as the inspiration for Lewis's Gopher Prairie. The citizens of Sauk Centre proudly renamed their main boulevard "The Original Main Street," while a cross street was renamed "Sinclair Lewis Avenue" in his honor.

"He was a literary sociologist who believed in seeing America first and knew his country better than most writers of his generation," wrote biographer Richard Lingeman, who also noted that writers such as James T. Farrell, John O'Hara and John Marquand claimed they'd learned their craft from Lewis.[96] John Updike, Lingeman said, reread *Babbitt* before creating his character Rabbit Angstrom in *Rabbit is Rich*. And Tom Wolfe, author of *Bonfire of the Vanities*, proclaimed, "If someone said to me, 'Okay, pick the greatest American novel of the 20th century,' I would pick *Elmer Gantry*. Lewis isn't a fashionable figure in American literature, but he's such [a] giant, and I think the reason is that he went out and looked at America."[97]

There was one Sinclair Lewis novel still waiting to be published—but first I had to write it. In 2009 my eldest son, Barnaby, also a writer and editor, was rooting through my files and dredged up a musty two-hundred page manuscript of *Thus Ever to Tyrants*, the story about John Wilkes Booth that Lewis had so vividly (if briefly) outlined over our early morning thermos of coffee in 1947. About a decade ago—at eighty!—I'd started it, but couldn't finish it. Though I'd published over thirty-five books in my lifetime, this story flummoxed me; my agent Don Congdon had sent it around, but no takers. "No market for old-fashioned stories," he'd said.

"Dad, it's a great tale," my son urged. "You've got to finish it."

Sixty years later Lewis's nagging voice resounded, "If you don't finish that Booth book, you'll never make a writer!" Thus began my challenge: To transform one of history's most reviled assassins into a sympathetic character.

I had to make the story my own. Instead of following Lewis's plan to exile Booth in the Midwest—a region that I knew little about—I sent the assassin out West, to Montana Territory in the summer of 1865. Booth narrowly evades capture and travels on a steamboat up the Missouri River to the frontier port of Fort Benton, a town of fur traders, muleskinners, post Indians, and outlaws. There he meets a good woman who redeems him...until the wheel of tragedy turns again. I chose Fort Benton because my grandfather, John Conrad, had migrated there from Virginia at fifteen in 1870. I knew Montana well from boyhood summers, and I'd later taken my children, all avid trout fishermen and history buffs, to explore The Last Best Place.

I thought of Red constantly as I rewrote the manuscript. Would he have approved of the scene where Booth joins up with photographer Mathew Brady to gain access to Robert E. Lee? Would he have liked the way I made Booth (who, at twenty-four, was a tremendous athlete) enter a local prize-fighting contest in St. Louis to earn boat passage up the Missouri? At a certain point, I had to push back against the ghost of my mentor, to write it my own way. Booth couldn't use his acting skills or someone might recognize him; so how would he earn a living in Fort Benton? He begins as a horse-breaker, only to be kicked in the head by a stallion. What next?

As a painter myself, it seemed natural that an actor with a knack for mimicry might turn to the smaller stage of a watercolor pad. So I had Booth aspiring to paint like George Catlin, selling souvenir sketches of the Blackfeet, antelope and grizzly bears to the gold seekers arriving by steamboat. I felt sure that Lewis would approve of Booth's unusual love interest, Fern—a stalwart but sensitive schoolteacher with a tragically scarred face who had been jilted as a mail-order bride. Yet I worried about Moody Suggs, Booth's eventual killer: Was he too broadly sketched as a drunken, unrepentant Southerner? Somehow, Red Lewis's ending for the novel—where Suggs shoots Booth as he portrays Lincoln—actually worked in this Wild West setting.

My son, Barnaby, who had just developed an imprint with Council Oak Books of Tulsa and San Francisco, bought the book. In May 2010, shortly after my eighty-eighth birthday, I began suffering from congestive heart failure. A few days later I entered Cottage Hospital in Santa Barbara for a six-hour surgery: a triple bypass and aortic valve replacement. Two weeks later I was home, reviewing galleys of *The Second Life of John Wilkes Booth*— my tenth novel and thirty-seventh book. Friends like Ray Bradbury, Joe Wambaugh, Sol Stein, Anthony Weller and T.C. Boyle gave it enthusiastic blurbs. The dedication reads: *For my mentor Sinclair Lewis, who told me this story so long ago.*

The Second Life was published in November 2010, and I waited for the reviews. As an old man watching the sand in the hourglass, I wanted very much to know that Sinclair Lewis's story had been worth a year of my life to write, rewrite—and rewrite again. The initial media response was sparse. Then Adam Nagourney, a reporter from *The New York Times*, called from Los Angeles. Instead of writing a conventional review, he wanted to interview me—as a literary antiquity, I suspected—at my beach house in Carpinteria.

On the appointed day, I waited in my cluttered studio, filled with memorabilia spanning seven decades. Faded bullfighting posters crowded my walls, their edges gnawed by my most recent parrot, an African Gray named Madison, who had recently been killed by a raccoon. Scattered on my desk were a framed letter from Steinbeck, snapshots of my children in the Sputnik era, and photos of long-dead bullfighters I'd known—including Manolete. (I'm a messy sort, but organized in my own way.) On the wall hung a framed 1915 letter from Theodore Roosevelt to my then recently-married mother. Above my desk was a color photograph of my oil portrait of Sinclair Lewis at his chessboard: The original was now in the Ransome Collection at the University of Texas. Nearby was the Booth book's original one-page literary contract that Lewis had typed-up and we both had signed on August 9, 1947.

I wondered what questions Nagourney would ask about Red Lewis, whom I hadn't seen since our disheartening Paris reunion in 1949. In those sixty-plus years, I had traveled the world, been gored (a second time) by a fighting bull, created a legendary nightclub, met movie stars and several Presidents, written bestsellers, owned a pet fox, painted hundreds of portraits, produced two prize-winning films, piloted seaplanes, lived in Tahiti for months with my first wife, started a writers' conference (now in its fortieth year) with my second wife, spent a life-saving month at the Betty Ford Clinic for alcoholism, gone on African safari, played elephant polo in Nepal, fathered four children I love dearly, trained several parrots to speak nearly as well as my kids, and taught two of my granddaughters to play the piano. In short, a lot of fun and adventure.

What, I suddenly thought, would Lewis say if he came back from the dead? "You should have written more books." *Writers—like us.*

Nagourney's thoughtful article appeared on a Wednesday in January 2011.[98] The next day a New York publisher called about the paperback rights to *Booth*, and on Friday someone from Harvey Weinstein's office inquired about the movie rights, but there was no follow-up to either call. The book shot up the Amazon rankings briefly, then subsided. Unlike the unexpected success with *Matador*, there were no over-stimulating telegrams—a method of communication as moribund as the manual typewriter rusting on my desk. Nevertheless, a few far-flung friends congratulated me by phone and letter, perhaps astonished that I was still alive! Then the world went back to doing whatever it was doing, and I went back to writing as best I could—this memoir of Red Lewis—and so much for his Booth idea. The contract was fulfilled.

What was the basic difference between Sinclair Lewis's life and mine? Aside from his far greater accomplishments, his life was not happy; while mine—in spite of the drinking, shock treatment, divorce, and rehab—was. And for that I'm grateful.

Writing is an exhilarating and humbling profession. Age and illness rarely help a writer, and right now, I'm not feeling so great. I know that my best work is behind me. I prefer to paint, even if I don't see as well as I used to. Still, on my ninetieth birthday, March 27, 2012, I had enough energy to play Fats Waller's "Alligator Crawl" on my daughter Tani's piano. My son Winston and his wife Paulette had flown in from Hawaii, while Barnaby and his wife Martha brought their toddler Jack out from Virginia. My daughters Kendall and Tani served a wonderful lunch for Mary and me. As my granddaughters Luisa and Fanny had a spirited go at the piano, I watched little Jack bob to the beat.

A good day all around. And now I'll take a nap before I rewrite the beginning of this memoir, again. *Writers—like us.*

EPILOGUE
By Barnaby Conrad III

My father died on February 12, 2013 at his home overlooking the Pacific Ocean near Carpinteria, California, just six weeks short of his ninety-first birthday.

After heart surgery in 2010, he bounced back to promote *The Second Life of John Wilkes Booth* on the Dennis Miller radio program, then flew up to San Francisco for a crowded book-signing event at Modernism Gallery in November. One of his old writer-friends, book editor and novelist Jack Leggett, who had guided *Matador* into print at Houghton Mifflin in 1952, showed up no worse for wear at age ninety-three.

Much of this short memoir of Sinclair Lewis, is based on three vivid chapters Dad wrote about Lewis in his 1969 memoir, *Fun While It Lasted.* Working together, we mined Mark Shorer's monumental biography (1961) and Richard Lingeman's more elegant portrait of Lewis (2002), as well as Ida Kay Compton's brief memoir, *Sinclair Lewis at Thorvale Farm.* Various libraries around the country provided letters by Lewis and others to illuminate details of the past. Little by little we fleshed-out the book.

By late 2012 it was an effort for Dad to make handwritten notes, so he dictated changes and additions to me. He was lucid enough to orally correct a few minor discrepancies when I visited him a week before he died. And then the story-telling stopped.

That summer at Thorvale with Sinclair Lewis shaped my father's life as a writer. I knew this even as a young boy when I asked about the startling portrait of the gaunt, red-faced author staring over a chessboard. Though Dad loved his own father, a kind-hearted businessman, Sinclair Lewis became his literary godfather, the mercurial Merlin who had magically passed along the secrets of the writer's craft.

Lewis and my father couldn't have been more different, yet they held great affection for each other. Lewis was quick to anger while my father avoided conflict and hurtful comments. They differed in social grace, looks, athletic abilities, and natural charm, but both were kind, sensitive men. Both were romantics at heart with little interest in modernism. They disliked bullies, rooted for the underdog, hated pomposity, and, though not really religious, they couldn't help wondering about the spiritual realm.

And they were both alcoholics. If my father hadn't stopped drinking for five crucial years in the 1980s, he might have died at the same age as Lewis (sixty-five). While Lewis was on the wagon, he would refuse a drink from a friend and mumble, "I used to be a drunk, you know." After doing the Betty Ford program in 1984, my father abstained for several crucial years and wrote *Time Is All We Have*, about his journey to sobriety. Gradually he became an on-and-off drinker, tapering in his last decade to the occasional glass of wine. He was lucky—and he lived twenty-four years longer than Lewis did.

While there may be a genetic proclivity to alcoholism, there is a less provable theory that writers (whether great, middling, or failed) are more prone to drinking than the average Joe or Jane. The American writers (Lewis, Faulkner, Hemingway and Steinbeck) who have won the Nobel Prize (or who might have, like Fitzgerald) could easily have drained a distillery. Writers see the world as it might have been, as it should be, or as it will never be—which can make it tough to live a normal life. As T.S. Eliot once wrote, "Humankind cannot bear very much reality."

Both Lewis and my father were gifted mimics and enjoyed hamming it up on stage—perhaps as a psychic release after hours of rewriting one chapter or just one obstinate page. They were truly fascinated with the unlimited peculiarities and quirks of their fellow earthlings. Both named Dickens among their favorite authors. Every day at the typewriter it was the best of times, and the worst of times.

Lewis was a compulsive genius who had few distractions, except chess and drinking, to divert his hyper-charged writer's mind, and he died alone. In contrast, my father had a full career as a portrait painter and artist, plus many serious hobbies like playing the piano, flying small aircraft, training parrots to speak, making prize-winning films, wood-carving, skeet-shooting, running a nightclub, playing tennis, flyfishing for trout, and teaching future writers. He generally liked people, and died gracefully at his home by the sea, surrounded by his wife and his four children.

Shortly after Dad's death, I pulled a green leather-bound book from my bookshelf. It was the copy of *Cass Timberlane* that Sinclair Lewis had inscribed to his young secretary in 1947: "For Barny Conrad, whom a summer at Thorvale has shown to be the most amiable man living." A dozen years ago, my father gave me that leather-bound volume and added his own dedication on a card: "This book means more to me than any other I've owned...Love and happy birthday! From Dad."

Well, Dad, you were the most amiable man in my world, and I treasure our sixty-one years together. *Vaya con Dios.*

ENDNOTES

[1] Chauncey Brewster Tinker (1876-1963), a popular Yale professor, translated *Beowulf* in 1910. In 1925 he was among the first to examine the historic James Boswell's papers at Malahide Castle in Ireland, later acquired by Colonel Ralph Heyward Isham and subsequently by Yale. Brewster retired from Yale in 1945.

[2] *Kingsblood Royal* would sell 1.5 million. Richard Lingeman, *Sinclair Lewis, Rebel from Main Street*, New York, Randon House, 2002, page 506.

[3] Marcella met Michael Amrine in 1940 in New Orleans. In 1950 he published *Secret*, a novel about the atomic bombing of Hiroshima.

[4] Ken Millar went on to a hugely successful career as Ross McDonald, creator of the "Lew Archer" detective series. His wife, Margaret Millar, wrote successful mystery novels.

[5] Dorothy Thompson: "My instantaneous reaction", Vincent Sheean, *Dorothy and Red*, Boston: Houghton Mifflin, 1963. Page 347.

[6] "If I ever divorce Dorothy" Vincent Sheean, *Dorothy and Red*, Boston: Houghton Mifflin, 1963. Page 263.

[7] "And thanks to you" Lewis letter to Powers, March 31, 1947. (St. Cloud State University Archives, St. Cloud, Minnesota).

[8] "I send you every most affectionate" Lewis letter to Powers. March 8, 1947 (St. Cloud State University Archives).

[9] Lewis met with black leaders like Walter White to research *Kingsblood Royal*. Lingeman, pages 500-503.

[10] Jane White's performance was reviewed in Eleanor Roosevelt's nationally syndicated newspaper column "My Day", December 12, 1945.

[11] "Wells Lewis had been" Wells Lewis's death, Lingeman, pages 485-486.

[12] "There was something almost" Thomas Wolfe, *You Can't Go Home Again*, Scribner, New York, page 464.

[13] List of alienated friends, Schorer, *Sinclair Lewis: An American Life*, page 804.

[14] "His copper-red hair…provincial." Lingeman, page 19.

[15] Yeats anecdote, Lingeman, page 19.

[16] "Was the only man at Yale" Lingeman, page 20.

[17] Selling story ideas to London, Lingeman, pages 37-38.

[18] Working for Upton Sinclair, Lingeman, pages 25-27.

[19] William H. Hunt's father, William Henry Hunt, had studied at Yale Law School in 1844; he served as President James Garfield's Secretary of the Navy, then as Minister to Russia, where he died in 1884.

[20] Barnaby Conrad III, *Ghost Hunting in Montana*, New York: Harper Collins West, 1994, pages 235-241.

[21] Lewis at his 1922 Reunion, Lingeman, pages 199-200.

[22] *History of the Class of 1907,* Yale University Press, New Haven, 1947.

[23] "Kingsblood", by Horace R. Cayton, *Pittsburgh Courier*, June 7, 1947, page 7.

[24] Jefferson Davis quote about Hiram Revels. Horace R. Cayton, *Long Old Road*, New York: Trident Press, 1965. page 6.

25 Horace Cayton and St. Clair Drake, *Black Metropolis: A Study of Negro Life in a Northern City*, Chicago: The University of Chicago Press, 1945.

[26] Although conversations like this took place, the author's memory was refreshed by Horace Cayton's book, *Long Old Road*, Chapter 13, pages 293-308.

[27] Horace Cayton, *Long Old Road*, ibid.

[28] Horace Cayton, *Long Old Road,* ibid.

[29] Orville Scott, *New York Times*, May 23, 1947, page 20.

[30] Clifton Fadiman, *Saturday Review,* May 24, 1947, pp. 9-10.

[31] "Hy Craft had adapted" Lingeman, page 51.

[32] *The God-Seeker,* Lingeman, pages 528.

[33] "From the Lobster Pot" Lewis letter to Marcella Powers, July 20, 1947.

[34] "Here, strengthened by their scholarly care" is from Lewis's poem "Hermit on a Florence Hill" written in May 1951, discovered after Lewis's death. Shorer, page 801.

[35] Dorothy Thompson's sex life, Sheean, *Dorothy & Red*, pages 239-40.

[36] Marcella and Lewis possibly lost a child, Lingeman, ibid, page 441.

[37] "a completely hollow creature" H.L. Mencken on Marcella Powers' looks and intelligence, Lingeman, page 441.

[38] "*Sic Semper Tyrannis*" "Thus Ever to Tyrants" was (and remains) the motto of the state of Virginia.

[39] "Portrait of Lewis", C.R.W. Nevinson (1889-1946), *Paint and Prejudice*. New York: Harcourt, Brace, 1938. Pages 236-38

[40] James Joyce anecdote, Bennett Cerf, *At Random*, pages 90-93.

[41] "Gertrude Stein, here you are" Bennett Cerf, *At Random*, page 103

[42] "Lewis flew through life" John Hersey, "My Summer Job with Sinclair Lewis", *New York Times,* May 10, 1987, Book Review, Section 7, page 36.

[43] "War loomed, he said." Hersey, ibid., page 38.

[44] "Barny! When will you learn" Entire conversation between Lewis and BC was recorded by Ida L. Compton in her memoir *Sinclair Lewis At Thorvale Farm*. Sarasota: Ruggles. 1988. Page 41.

[45] "Not only can it" Walter White, *Chicago Daily News*, Aug. 16, page 6, col. 3.

[46] "This reduces to" Walter White, *Chicago Daily News*, ibid.

[47] In fact, Lewis hired an earnest grad student from the Midwest, James Roers, but banished him to New York City to do research. Lingeman, page 520.

[48] "Your letter sounds as tho" Letter from Lewis to Conrad, Oct. 14, 1947.

[49] "I'm a little concerned" Letter from Lewis to Conrad, Nov. 30, 1947.

[50] "After much meditation" Letter from Lewis to Conrad, ibid.

[51] "I take it that" Letter from Lewis to Conrad, 1948, whereabouts unknown.

[52] "But Barnaby" Letter from Ida Kay Compton to Conrad, Schorer, page 768.

[53] Letter from Lewis to Conrad, whereabouts unknown.

[54] "He had probably never worked so hard" Schorer, page 768.

[55] "Out of the limbo" F. Cordasco, *Brooklyn Daily Eagle*, July 19, 1948, page 12.

[56] Charles Poore, *New York Times,* Saturday, June 19, 1948, page 13.

[57] "Red spent his last night" Bennett Cerf, *At Random*, 1977, page 146-147.

[58] "After absence" Lewis to Ida Kay Compton, January 2, 1949 (St. Cloud State University Archives.)

[59] "It's an enchanted colony" Lewis to Ida Kay Compton, Feb. 11, 1949 (St. Cloud State University Archives.)

[60] "Berenson had heard" Shorer, page 775.

[61] "Mrs. Powers is amazingly happy" Lewis to Ida Kay Compton, Jan. 18, 1949 (St. Cloud State University Archives.)

[62] "This couple, blast them, are so charming" Lewis to Ida Kay Compton, Feb. 11, 1949 (St. Cloud State University Archives.)

[63] "I love America" Perry Miller, "The Incorruptible Sinclair Lewis," *Atlantic Monthly*, April 1951. page 34. (quoted in Lingeman.)

[64] "The mother very neat and well washed" Ernest Hemingway letter to Charles Scribner, July 22, 1949. *Ernest Hemingway, Selected Letters*, Scribners, 1981, page 60.

[65] "His face was a piece of old liver" Mary Welsh Hemingway, *How it Was*, Alfred A. Knopf, Inc., 1971, page 234.

[66] "How the hell could I write" Hemingway to Charles Scribner, ibid (July 22, 1949.)

[67] "They looked at the man" Hemingway, *Across The River and Into the Trees*, New York: Scribners, 1950, page 78.

[68] "Despite all apostolic warnings" Lewis to Conrad, March 3, 1949. (Whereabouts of letter unknown.)

[69] "One hurt, wounded" Ida Kay Compton to Conrad Nov. 8, 1977 (St. Cloud State University Archives).

[70] "That night Red" Ida Kay Compton to Conrad Nov. 8, 1977, ibid.

[71] "Finally, in desperation" Ida Kay Compton to Conrad, ibid.

[72] "Darling, you have" Ida Kay Compton, *Sinclair Lewis at Thorvale Farm,* page 50.

[73] "God, Ida, I can think of hundreds" Ida Kay Compton, *Sinclair Lewis at Thorvale Farm*, page 50

[74] "I've given my life" (Red) Ida Kay Compton, *Sinclair Lewis at Thorvale Farm*, page 51.

[75] "Garçong! Come here, you bloody garçong!" Lingeman, *Sinclair Lewis*, page 181, quoting Malcolm Cowley in Brentano's *Book Chat,* May/June 1927, page 26.

[76] "that worn-out old expatriate", Michael Lewis on James Campbell, cited in Schorer, page 796.

[77] "as far as possible from the Dôme and other haunts of Harold Stearns", Lewis to H.L. Mencken, cited in Schorer, page 409.

[78] "Did see Barney (sic)", Lewis to Ida Kay Compton, October 26/27, 1949, St. Cloud University Library Archives)

[79] Alexander ("Alec") Manson, Schorer, page 787.

[80] "No one has ever" Lewis telling Campbell, in Lingeman, page 538. From Campbell interview with Mark Shorer, MS papers (Bancroft Library, University of California, Berkeley)

[81] "Alexander Manson is the only good secretary" Lewis to Ida Kay Compton, February 1, 1950. (Collection St. Cloud State University)

[82] Dr. Vincenzo Lapiccirella: "Only geniuses and kings" Lingeman, page 538.

[83] "Europe is home to me" Lewis to Ida Kay. Ida Kay Compton, 1951. Schorer, page 803.

[84] "Alec, something terrible" Alexander Manson as told to Helen Camp, "The Last Days of Sinclair Lewis," *The Saturday Evening Post*, March 31, 1951, 27, 110-112.

[85] "In the bitter cold" to Ida Kay, Ida Kay Compton, *Sinclair Lewis at Thorvale Farm*, page 18.

[86] "I have been thinking" Conrad to Ida Kay Compton, Feb. 5., 1951. (St. Cloud State University Archives)

[87] "More than a novel" Victor Hass *Chicago Tribune*, June 9, 1952, page 149.

[88] Walter Kerr, *The Herald Tribune*, Sept. 25, 1963.

[89] Howard Taubman, *The New York Times*, Sept. 25, 1963.

[90] "Red's will was interesting" Harrison Smith to Conrad, August 7, 1951.

[91] "Red was the most courageous," Powers letter (circa 1985) to Isabel Lewis Agrell, published in Agrell's memoir *Sinclair Lewis Remembered*, page 68. Privately Printed, 1996.

[92] Michael Lewis, Lingeman, page 550.

[93] "He was one of the worst writers in modern American literature," Schorer, ibid, page 813.

[94] "Sinclair Lewis seems" Gore Vidal, "The Romance of Sinclair Lewis," *New York Review of Books,* Oct. 8, 1992.

[95] "he created no school of writing" Grace Hegger Lewis, *With Love from Gracie, Sinclair Lewis 1912-1915. New York: Harcourt, Brace & Co., 1951, page 133.*

[96] "He was a literary sociologist" Lingeman, page 553.

[97] "If someone said to me," Bob Luncergaard, "Novelist Tom Wolfe Says His Hero is Sinclair Lewis," Minneapolis *Star-Tribune*, April 14, 1988.

[98] Adam Nagourney, "A Promise Kept to Sinclair Lewis," *The New York Times*, January 26, 2011.

SELECTED BIBLIOGRAPHY

Baker, Carlos, ed. *Ernest Hemingway: Selected Letters, 1917-1961*. New York: Scribners, 1981.

Cayton, Horace and Drake, St. Clair and, *Black Metropolis*. Chicago: University of Chicago, 1945.

Cayton, Horace. *Long Old Road*. New York: Trident Press, 1965

Compton, Ida Kay. *Sinclair Lewis at Thorvale Farm*. Sarasota: Ruggles, 1988.

Conrad, Barnaby. *Dangerfield*. New York: Harper and Row, 1961.

Conrad, Barnaby. *Fun While It Lasted*. New York: Random House, 1969.

Conrad, Barnaby. *Name Dropping: Tales From my Barbary Coast Saloon*. New York: HarperCollinsWest, 1994.

Hemingway, Ernest, *Across the River and Into the Trees*. New York: Scribners, 1950.

Lewis, Grace Hegger, *With Love from Gracie, Sinclair Lewis 1912-1915. New York: Harcourt, Brace and Company, 1951.*

Lingeman, Richard. *Sinclair Lewis: Rebel From Main Street*. New York: Random House, 2002.

Scharnhorst, Gary and Hofer, Matthew, ed. *Sinclair Lewis Remembered*. Tuscaloosa: The University of Alabama Press, 2012.

Schorer, Mark. *Sinclair Lewis: An American Life*. New York: McGraw-Hill, 1961.

Schulberg, Budd. *The Four Seasons of Success*. New York: Doubleday, 1972.

Sheean, Vincent. *Dorothy and Red*. Boston: Houghton Mifflin, 1963.

Van Doren, Carl. *Sinclair Lewis: A Biographical Sketch*. Garden City, N.Y.: Doubleday, Doran, 1933.

www.ingramcontent.com/pod-product-compliance
Lightning Source LLC
Chambersburg PA
CBHW060416100426
42812CB00037B/3490/J